LIVE
RAW

RAW FOOD RECIPES FOR GOOD HEALTH AND TIMELESS BEAUTY

LIVE
RAW

RAW FOOD RECIPES FOR GOOD HEALTH AND TIMELESS BEAUTY

Mimi Kirk

Skyhorse Publishing

contents

INTRODUCTION viii

Introduction

I was born in Hollywood, California, in 1938, the youngest of seven children. My mother outlived four of my siblings and my father by thirty years. I grew up in less than a middle-class family and far from a glamorous life. My sweet mother was a simple cook and we rarely went out to eat, so I didn't learn much about food growing up.

I was married at seventeen and was widowed at twenty-nine; I am the mother of two girls and two boys and grandmother of seven children.

Before my husband died in a private plane crash February of 1968, I was a stay-at-home mom. I quickly realized we had no insurance or financial savings, and I had to find a job very quickly to support my family. Three months after his death and four months before my thirtieth birthday, a producer friend helped me get a job as a screen extra in the movie industry and gave me a small speaking part in one of his television movies. In 1970, while working at Paramount Studios, producer James L. Brooks discovered me. Brooks thought I resembled the star of his upcoming television series, *The Mary Tyler Moore Show,* and arranged a meeting between Mary and me. She hired me on the spot as her stand-in.

Because of my original style of dressing, I worked with Valerie Harper designing a good deal of her wardrobe and I created the famous headscarf she wore on *Rhoda.* Throughout my entertainment career of eighteen years, I also worked in front of the camera on numerous television shows and movies.

I started my spiritual path in 1969 when a friend told me about meditation and thought it would be a good way to heal from the loss of my husband. Meditation helped ease the pain and gave me strength. It opened the doors of knowledge to the ebb and flow of life and inspired me to live more in the moment. I always felt meditation was like learning a secret about life that not many people knew about. It was exciting and fulfilling and influenced my path in life. My children enjoyed going to services with me and loved to sit in a peaceful little meditation room I made under a stairwell in our home. I was blessed to study with two living gurus: Swami Prabhavananda of Vedanta Society and, later, after his death in 1976, Swami Muktananda of Siddah Yoga.

In 1980, when my oldest children were grown and out on their own, my youngest daughter, Mia, and I went to Swami Muktananda's ashram in South Fallsburg, New York, for several months to study with him. Later, after his passing, I traveled to Ganeshpuri, India, and studied in my guru's ashram with his successor, a woman known as Swami Chidvilasananda. This is the same ashram Elizabeth Gilbert lived at for a short time and mentions in her book *Eat, Pray, Love.*

After leaving the film industry in 1984, I became an entrepreneur. I designed and manufactured costume jewelry under my spiritual name "Prasuti" Accessories. (*Prasuti* means "mother of divine children" in Hindu terms.) After selling my company in early 1986, I took a job in Beverly Hills as majordomo for a wealthy family, overseeing all aspects of their estate and helping to create and implement many charitable events. It was a very exciting time, with many formal parties and events, European travel, private planes, yachts, and a taste of the rich and famous lifestyle.

My environmental concerns became very strong, and after three years, I left my job there to create, publish, and edit the *City Planet,* an environmental newspaper in Los Angeles. I later moved to Taos, New Mexico, to find the "simple life" and, while there, helped start the city's first film festival. I worked with several local nonprofits to help raise money and awareness about health and environmental concerns. In 1998, I created the first board game specifically geared toward women entitled Cowgirls Ride the Trail of Truth, and in 2000, I authored the book *Cowgirl Spirit.* This is only a small part of my many incarnations, including a short stint as a Las Vegas showgirl at the Flamingo Hotel in 1957. The rest of my life would make a book all by itself.

My family is the most important to me. I have a very close relationship with my children and grandchildren. I am in a wonderful eight-year relationship with a man almost twenty years my junior.

Two years ago, I sold my cowgirl company and retired. I now spend much of my time tending my award-winning cactus and vegetable garden and traveling with my boyfriend. I lecture, give live-food demonstrations, and manage my ever-growing online social network, which includes thousands around the world. I am passionate about helping others attain a healthier lifestyle and share what I've experienced in my many years here on earth. If this book helps one person who needs a lift, I'm happy.

WHERE I AM TODAY

Winning PETA's nationwide contest for the title "Sexiest Vegetarian Over 50" was quite a thrill. For me, being sexy has to do with being happy with myself inside and out. Having sex appeal is about energy and vigor, and being kind and compassionate to all living things.

Every day I realize how blessed I am to be healthy and to have gained the knowledge to stay healthy. At my age, I know that life without good health can be complicated. There are health risks when having Botox injections, plastic surgery, and artificial procedures, and besides the health risks, I have friends who've had procedures and turned out looking stiff and unnatural. There is no point in having perfect breasts, an unlined face, or a flat stomach if you are not in good health.

Because I am healthy, there is no need to stop dreaming and having goals. I hope to see my family grow, my grandchildren become parents, and maybe even my great-great-grandchildren graduate from college. I want to accomplish more in my life and try new things I've never done. I don't think about what I can't do at my age; I think about what I can do. I see myself as a work in progress.

Whether you're new to raw foods, a longtime advocate, high raw, vegetarian, vegan, or a carnivore, I hope *Live Raw* will inspire you to take a look at improving your health. If we make the conscious choice to celebrate our life and the life of our planet by ridding ourselves of foods and lifestyles that do not support us, I believe we can live in harmony and enjoy a long, healthy, happy, productive life—and look good doing it!

If you prepare food for yourself, your family, or a house full of friends, raw food will put a smile on surprised faces. There is nothing like fresh, juicy raw food to make you feel sexy and alive.

Raw food preparation is an art, but it can be as easy as you want. Once you decide to eat healthier, you will learn to make the most delicious dishes you've ever tasted. *Live Raw* is filled with fantastic recipes. You may not recognize some of the tools and ingredients at first, but soon, like I did, you will feel as though you've known them forever.

In the early '70s I decided to give up eating animals and become a vegetarian. I was returning to the *Mary Tyler Moore* set after picking up some sliced roast beef for lunch. I reached over on the passenger seat where the package was sitting to take a small piece to munch on. As I began to chew the meat, I thought I took a bite out of the back of my hand. I realized I was chewing flesh. That did it. I was sick to my stomach. That was the very moment I decided to give up eating animals and become a vegetarian. It was a spiritual choice; I did not want to kill animals to eat.

Soon after, I learned about the cruelty farm animals endure. Being compassionate was high on my list of important things to do. Being a vegetarian did not mean I gave up processed foods like cookies, chips, or other foods considered not so healthy, but I knew I was doing the right thing for my young family's health and the health of animals by adopting a vegetarian lifestyle.

There wasn't much information around at that time, and since I was brought up with the notion that meat was the major source of protein, I had a lot to learn about feeding my family properly so they would get the nourishment they needed.

I also started to become aware of the environmental issues facing our planet. It is widely agreed millions of forests are destroyed to house cattle, and millions more to raise grain to feed the cattle. Experts say it takes seven pounds of grain and soybean protein to produce one pound of meat protein. If the same land were used to produce food for humans directly, seven times more people could eat. Many like myself agree that eating animals impedes spiritual development and is a violent disruption of the inner spirit. I adopted these beliefs long before publishing my environmental newspaper in 1989.

It's time to change the way we eat. If we're not going to do it for our own health, it needs to be done to help take pressure off the environment. Yet many people find change difficult, even in the face of the environmental problems, such as deforestation in the Amazon rain forest. To be exact, 232,000 square miles of Amazon rain forest have been destroyed since 1970. Central America, Costa Rica, and Brazil are heading in the same direction. The idea of giving up anything we love—and anything that, on the surface, doesn't appear to hurt others—seems ridiculous. Who wants to tackle a new way of living or eating, especially for a vague reason like, "It's good for you"? But then the problem will only get worse, until suddenly, it'll be right up in your face.

We want to feel our best, especially as we age. In 2007, I was told my blood pressure was up. I was starting to feel little arthritis pains in my joints. Since I've always had good health, this served as a real wake-up call to me. I had recently gained about twenty pounds impressing my boyfriend with my cooking skills. I'd even gone so far as to pack boxes of clothes in the garage, waiting for me to lose the weight.

My family health history wasn't exactly rosy. There's been a bit of everything including high blood pressure, high cholesterol, cancer, diabetes, heart attacks, strokes, asthma, leukemia, and Parkinson's. I could go on, but you get the picture, and so did I. This was not the path I wanted to go down. I knew I had to step up my game if I wanted to avoid future health problems and follow in my family's footsteps. This was when I started researching what foods contained which nutrients and vitamins to keep different parts of the body healthy.

I've never been as excited about an eating lifestyle in all my forty years as a health advocate as I am about raw food. I will teach you how to eat in a way that helps save the animals and the planet, and keep you youthful and healthy. And for all you foodies out there like me, this food is gourmet, tasty, and totally gorgeous.

I feel better than ever. I'm in the best shape of my life. No, I don't have the "perfect body" as defined by models in magazines, but then most of us never like our bodies no matter how close to the ideal we get. At my age, I'm thrilled with the way I look and feel. I have energy all day long and well into the wee hours of the night. I'm in love with everything and everyone around me. My skin, hair, and nails have the look and feel of someone much younger than my age. I was told long ago by many older women, "Everything changes when you age. Your health deteriorates, your looks go, your energy level is low, and you are not quite as excited about things as you used to be." I'm here to dispel these myths.

Plain and simple, "Eat healthy foods for a healthy lifestyle." What I'm going to share with you in my book will hopefully get you started in the right direction toward a healthier, happier life regardless of age.

Many people seem to think medication is the only way to cure diseases. Many just sigh and willingly accept the notion that heredity plays the largest part in determining their health. Many try surgery and drastic beauty treatments to hold on to their looks. Not so! I believe we can heal ourselves and stay healthy well into our later years with good nutrition, exercise, positive attitude, love, and compassion.

I know this works because I've experienced it personally. I cured myself of arthritis joint pains and I'm controlling my blood pressure. I have the energy of someone in her twenties, and if I must say so myself, I'm looking pretty good for a woman my age.

Try my suggestions and recipes, and I think you will be quite surprised how quickly your health will improve and how much energy you'll have. You will naturally control your body weight without even thinking about it. You will hop out of bed without aches or pains. You will like what you see in the mirror, and you will feel different emotionally and physically—almost like you did in childhood.

I've chosen to eat organic raw vegan food because of my compassion for animals and its health benefits. Little did I know at the time that a raw-food way of eating would include all my favorite foods! Eating organic, live, plant-based food is known to have more nutrition than conventionally grown food. It has fewer chemicals and carcinogens than packaged food or animal products.

FOOD AND ROMANCE

Love—it's the subject of songs, paintings, movies, poetry, literature . . . and food.

Food is sexy to me. I love watching a seedling push its way up through the soil, hearing a snap when cutting open a cold crisp watermelon, or inhaling the citrus fragrance after peeling an orange. I become enchanted with possibilities just looking at food in the raw.

Eating freshly picked, uncooked, unprocessed fruits and vegetables in their natural state is the best food choice we can make for our health. Although I could tell you to eat a whole apple, a handful of nuts, or a chopped-up cucumber and leave it at that, I think it's a lot more exciting to create satisfyingly yummy meals out of these same ingredients. In my book, I'll show you how fantastically delicious and healthy raw food can be with just a little bit of coaxing.

I consider myself a gourmet foodie of sorts. Truth be told, I could live on luscious salads and green drinks, but I also want to create gorgeous, healthy meals for my family, my friends, and myself. There are times in my kitchen when I want to throw caution to the wind and toss around some herbs and spices while listening to salsa music on my iPod. Raw food preparation is an art, and when I'm in my kitchen, I feel like an artist.

Some of you may already know the joys of eating a plant-based raw food diet, but for those who don't, once you start eating more raw food, you will quickly see your health, looks, and attitude change for the better. Needless to say, you will fall in love . . . with yourself.

To love oneself is the beginning of a lifelong romance.

—Oscar Wilde (1854–1900)

CHAPTER 1

. . . .

THE PLEASURE OF FEELING

GOOD

. . . .

It's time for you to get started on improving your health and have fun doing it. It's time to stop taking food for granted and have a better relationship with it. It's time to fall in love with your body and let it know you care. Romance is in the air, and it's yours for the taking.

A person too busy to take care of his or her health is like a mechanic too busy to take care of his own car. Make time for yourself. Toss out everything in your kitchen that does not serve you in having better health. Empty your cupboards and refrigerator and restock them with foods that are committed to bringing you nutrition.

If you've ever even flirted with trying raw food, take the plunge: try a green juice or smoothie, look at it like a first date. If the smoothie makes you feel good, try a second one. Raw food can be an experience of love at first sight, and for others it may take some courting. If you give yourself fully to the experience, it will be a rewarding journey of self-awareness and extremely good health.

You can change one meal at a time. Replace one cooked meal with one raw meal. Find a recipe in the book that reminds you of an old favorite and try my raw version. Take your time or go all the way—it's up to you. However, once you are grounded in self-love, taking better care of yourself will just come naturally. When you learn to make a few raw food dishes, many mysteries of raw food preparation will unravel and the whole process will seem quite easy.

Once you've fallen in love with raw food, be kind to others who haven't made the leap. Allow them their opinions but don't let it affect how you are feeling or what you are doing for yourself. People learn not by what you say, but by the examples they see. When friends and family notice you have more energy, have lost unwanted pounds, rid yourself of medication, and look younger, they will take more interest in what you are doing.

Educate yourself by reading and meeting others who enjoy extraordinary good health and feel younger every day by eating raw foods. Conflicts may arise, so don't expect that you will never disagree, be confused, or have some not-so-raw moments.

It's not a bad thing; sometimes we learn more from what doesn't work than from what does.

Falling in love with healthy eating habits is rare. For those of us who have, it's a wonderful state to be in. When you find the "one way" to eat that is both healthy and satisfying, unwanted weight will drop off. You will get stronger, want to exercise more often, and you will walk around with a smile on your face—like when you are in love. Changing your health will be an inspiration to others. Show your body love by eating the right food, and it will take care of you in your old age.

what raw food means

Raw food is not "rabbit food." We eat more than carrots and celery. Raw food includes fruits, vegetables, nuts, seeds, sprouts, grains, seaweed, spices, herbs, oils, and sweeteners, all in combinations that excite the palate. Raw food is uncooked, unprocessed, and organic. It can be dehydrated, fermented, sprouted, and sundried. The variety of taste, textures, and colors is endless. Raw food is not always eaten cold. A dehydrator can be used to warm foods and you can also heat in your Vita-Mix blender, but I find it can easily overheat that way. At times I heat soup in a double boiler on the stove, but only enough to make it slightly warm so as not to destroy the enzymes.

BENEFITS OF RAW FOODS

Raw food creates major health improvements. Weight normalizes, energy perks up, skin glows, and digestion gets better. You will feel and look younger, be happier, and appreciate life. Many processed foods have no nutritional value at all! They are loaded with fats, sugars, sodium, preservatives, and chemicals. Nearly every food found in a can, box, or pouch contains some type of preservative with a high salt content. Read the labels on everything you purchase that may be packaged. The only labels on fresh produce should read "organic" or "conventionally grown."

When you cook food over 118°F, the heat can essentially "cook" important vitamins and minerals, particularly enzymes, which are critical to helping the body absorb nutrients. In *Enzyme Nutrition*, Dr. Edward Howell, the first researcher to recognize the importance of the enzymes in food to human nutrition, said, "Whenever food is heated, enzymes are lost and denatured. Uncooked plant foods are rich in enzymes, which are needed for the digestive system to work properly." Enzymes help break down food particles quickly so the body can process them. Cooked food, on the other hand, passes through the digestive tract more slowly, allowing for fermentation and toxins to remain in the body. Toxins in the body can cause many problems, including hormonal turmoil, fatigue, arthritis, intestinal discomfort, skin eruptions, headaches, and much more. Fruits and vegetables are full of enzymes and the main reason raw food works so well on the system.

If you are trying to lose weight, it's best not to consume too much oil or nuts. Use your best judgment, though. It's better to have a handful of almonds daily than a slice of raw cheesecake every day. It's better to eat more greens, fruits, vegetables, and salads with occasional "special" heavier foods. When I first started eating raw food, I wanted more crackers, breads, desserts, and nut dishes, but after a while I seemed to crave lighter foods. These "special" raw food recipes are good to keep you on track. Without them, it would be easy to consume cooked or processed foods to satisfy your cravings.

EATING RAW FOOD DOES NOT STOP YOU FROM ENJOYING LIFE

You can still dine out, travel, enjoy delicious food, and entertain. You can chose to be high-raw, which means you get the majority of your calories from raw food (75% or more of your food comes from consuming raw foods), supplemented with a small amount of cooked grains or lightly steamed greens.

It might take some time to get into the rhythm of preparing raw food, but it will be time well spent. Don't give it all up if you don't have time to do everything. Don't be hard on yourself if you break some rules.

Smoothies, juices, salads, and fruits are my mainstay. It gets easier to know what your body is asking for after eating raw food for a while. I remember when I first started eating raw food I craved chocolate on a daily basis, but now I only eat it once in a while, and when I do, I only require a small amount to be satisfied.

Organization is important both in the kitchen and when doing weekly shopping. When I use my dehydrator, I try to make bread and crackers at the same time. The ingredients used on a daily basis are at my fingertips, and my blender, juicer, and food processor are on my countertop.

I know many women and men who want to adopt a raw food diet, but their mates are not interested. Many raw food enthusiasts have faced the same issues and have overcome them, and so will you.

Make your health a priority and everything will fall into place. Be patient with yourself and others around you.

Make your kitchen a fun place. I know in the beginning it can be work learning to prepare something new. By taking it slowly, in no time you will look forward to preparing food that nourishes you and your family.

Changing the way you eat will absolutely change the way you feel and look. It happened to me and to thousands of others who have incorporated a plant-based diet into their lives. It can happen to you once you decide to embrace a healthy eating style and a desire to feel energized and joyful. I feel eating healthy is the best way to show yourself some love.

Like many of us, I've been in and out of "diets" much of my life, even while following a vegetarian diet for the better part of forty years. It was very easy for me to eat a vegetarian diet and still gain weight. Pastas, desserts, starches, and processed foods were all part of my daily eating plan. But when I discovered raw, vegan, plant-based food, things drastically changed for me in every way.

I don't especially like the word "diet" because it has always held a negative connotation. It makes me feel like I would be deprived of things I enjoyed eating and I would be denied gastronomic pleasures, which would make me quite grumpy. So I don't really like to call raw food a diet. To me it's a way of living, a holistic lifestyle that goes along with compassion for animals, positive thinking, and concerns for our environment. For me it is the fountain of youth, a miracle. After eating a raw diet for only a short time, I started to look years younger than my age and felt the happiness and enthusiasm I enjoyed in my youth. In a short time, experimenting with beautiful organic produce, seeds, nuts, and spices allowed me to recreate a healthy raw version of any food I desired.

Even better, the raw food diet eliminated my "age"-related symptoms. Many raw food enthusiasts have also reported the following benefits of a raw food lifestyle:

- Stubborn weight is lost and not regained.
- Depression disappears.
- Soft skin and clear complexion is noticed within weeks.
- Need for over-the-counter drugs for headaches is eliminated.
- A joyful attitude is attained.
- Energy is increased.
- Digestion improves.
- The mind thinks more clearly and focus is improved.
- One becomes better in tune with the body's needs.
- Risk of diseases, including diabetes, heart disease, cancer, arthritis, high blood pressure, and cholesterol, is reduced.

One of the first steps in adopting a more plant-based lifestyle is having the desire to become healthier, feel better, and look better. I've heard many people say, "I want to change, but I don't have time to take care of myself. I'm busy with a job, family, or school." What good is the money you are working for if later in life you are sick and spend it all on doctors and drugs? Airplane safety rules state, "Put your oxygen mask on first, before assisting others." See where you can apply this analogy to your own situation.

You've got to be smart. Rushing around, skipping breakfast or lunch, grabbing a bite at a fast-food restaurant, having a big lunch . . . none of this is healthy. Take the time to plan your lunch and eat properly, and you won't be left wondering why you're gaining weight, feeling exhausted, and continually dieting. Grabbing a coffee in the morning might give you an immediate lift, but in the long run, it depletes your body of nutrients and adds nothing to your overall health and welfare. It's a momentary and unhealthy fix. What to do? A green drink with all the nutrients and life-giving vitamins will start your day off on the right note. Find out more about green drinks, including recipes for juices, smoothies, and detoxifying (see pages 65–88).

ONE FOOT IN FRONT OF THE OTHER

Many people shorten their lifespan and lower their resistance to stressful situations by eating foods that have little or no enzyme value. I want you to know this fact so you have a choice about what you eat. Processed foods do not contain live enzymes, which your body requires. In fact, processed foods contain refined sugars, extra salt, and other enhancers that could actually deplete you.

Although I believe raw food is the greatest way to eat for optimum health, I am not suggesting you switch to a 100 percent raw food diet immediately like I did and many others have. What I do think is important is to start including more raw foods into your daily diet, along with a morning "green drink." For some people it is easy to go 100 percent raw, for others a slower transition works best, and for still others, partially raw works best for them. A "green" juice or smoothie is a good place to start because they are such powerful healers, are great tasting, and are easy and quick to make. "Green" drinks definitely put a spring in your step and add years to your life.

The first question anyone asks me when they hear I'm a vegan is, "How do you get your protein?" Proteins, minerals, and vitamins can be obtained from a properly crafted diet of dark leafy greens, nuts, seeds, fruits, sea vegetables, and sprouts. Based on seven hundred studies, including Dr. Colin Campbell's *The China Study*, we need only 5–6 % of total calorie intake to replace the protein regularly excreted by the body. Multiple studies show that eating vegan protein is much healthier for us than animal protein. If you consume a green drink daily or a large salad containing greens, you will easily fulfill your protein needs. Spinach contains 49% protein; broccoli, 45%; lettuce, 34%; kale, 45%; Chinese cabbage, 34%; and sprouts like mung beans, 43%. Greens are higher in protein than fruits or nuts, but both are good sources of protein along with hemp seeds. An added bonus of vitamin, minerals, anticancer properties are also in these dark leafy greens.

For those who want to live a compassionate life, contribute to world peace and improve the environment, books including *The World Peace Diet* by Will M. Tuttle, *Eating Animals* by Jonathan Safran Foer, and *The China Study* by Dr. T. Collin Campbell are important to read. If you are already a vegetarian, you will be amazed at how much better you will feel if you become a vegan not only for moral reasons, but for your health as well.

don't be fearful of aging, there is hope

I don't want to achieve immortality through my work; I want to achieve immortality through not dying.
—Woody Allen

Young people think that getting older means the good times are over. The older you are, the more likely your doctor is going to prescribe a pill to help a problem rather than suggest you change your habits. Life is a cycle and I can't change my age, but being in the latter part of life doesn't mean there is not a lot of life yet to be lived.

Few people die of old age. Most die because of illness or accident or extreme cold or heat. As one ages, the ability to respond quickly is important. Can you move swiftly to avoid an accident? Can you catch yourself when tripping or falling down the stairs? Is your mind alert to obstacles on the road when you are walking or driving?

How can we age gracefully, look and feel younger than our actual years, and have optimum health without drugs or plastic surgery? How do we stay in top physical, mental, and emotional health? The simple answer is diet, exercise, and a positive mental attitude.

Eat well, keep fit, and along the way, be kind about how you look. It's easy to find fault with our aging bodies. You know the phrase, "The mirror doesn't lie"? We spend time looking in a magnifying mirror checking out the things on our face we don't like. As we age, we need to learn self-love. It's a time to see what is beautiful about our self, both from the outside and the inside. Those little laugh lines on our faces can be seen as a wonderful happy life that has been lived. What others perceive of us is what comes from inside, and then we outwardly reflect a healthy body and the joy of self-love.

It's time to decide if you want to regenerate or degenerate your body by what you eat and how you live. Once you learn how to do this, you can make informed choices on a daily basis. It's time for self-realization, not self-destruction. It's time to use all the wisdom and gifts you've gathered throughout your life. It's time to focus on your health and well-being and live the balance of your life joyful and active.

Your openness and willingness to take responsibility for your own health will lead you to a new exciting world that will change your life forever. Changes in mind, body, and spirit are always constant. You have the remote control in your hand, and I'm going to introduce you to some new channels and some new ways to rejuvenate yourself naturally.

Research and development in the medical field is constantly changing and new findings are presented daily. Recent studies from researchers at Boston University estimate that by the year 2030, aging baby boomers will join the ranks of centenarians, making the count of those living to be 100 or older in the millions worldwide. According to the United States Census Bureau, there are approximately five hundred thousand centenarians living around the world today. Good genes are certainly part of this, but as you know, I think other factors play a role.

Most centenarians believe that their diets, along with moderate exercise, play a major role in their longevity. It might be an incentive to eat for nutrition and not strictly for entertainment, but if it can maintain your mobility and memory, getting to 100 might be a pretty good goal.

Besides eating the proper diet and maintaining the proper weight, you need to be active, both mentally and physically. Simple things like walking thirty minutes and stretching daily can add years to your life. Gardening, lifting things that seem slightly heavy, using weights, or walking up and down the stairs can keep you fit. Reading, doing

crossword puzzles, staying involved, and finding your passion can also prolong life. Add good friends and family to the mix and you most likely will live longer. Be happy and enjoy life, maintain a positive attitude, and love where you are at each moment. When you feel healthy and happy, you look younger.

A simple secret to antiaging is to accept and appreciate yourself just the way you are. As you work on gaining better eating habits and including more exercise in your daily life, remember to do nice things for yourself. Get a massage or facial, take a walk in a beautiful location, go to a museum, go dancing, and be sure to walk barefoot on the sand or lawn. Learn to appreciate and look at nature in all its beauty, and it will reflect in your face, just as Mother Nature intended.

If you want to look young and thin, hang out with people older and fatter.

—Anonymous

body, mind, and spirit

You might not choose what is happening to you at any given moment, but *you can* choose to feel the way you want about the experience you are having. *You can* decide what to eat or what not to eat. *You can* decide what to think or what not to think. *You* are writing your own script for your own life. It's all up to you. You can't blame your circumstances, parents, family members, husband, friends, or boss.

When I awake in the morning, before I open my eyes, I take a quick moment to consciously think about how I would like my day to look. I don't know all the details, but what I do know is this: I want to do good things for my body to keep it healthy; I want to think positive and calm about any situation; I want to have fun, laugh, love, and make a difference in the lives that I touch that day. It seems simple enough, but it takes remembrance throughout the day. When I close my eyes at night, I set myself up for good dreams and happy thoughts. Think of the mind as a muscle; you must work it every day to gain strength.

MY BODY

I make choices daily to eat raw food because I feel healthy eating this way. I function at a very high level, I am happy, I attract good things into my life, and I'm enjoying myself. Is it raw food, you might ask? For me, I believe it is the main factor. When you feel healthy, you can handle any situation better. You think more clearly, your energy is better, and the smile on your face reflects it all. I've lived a full life, tried many modalities, and this seems to work best for me.

MY MIND

I don't like drama in my life. Or I say I don't like negative drama. I'm a dramatic person for sure; I look at life with excitement. I love to make life a party and I love to be surrounded by simple beauty. I love nature, art, people, and animals. I don't like arguing, being mean, selfish, or judgmental. I love peace. Staying realistic about any situation and not overdramatizing keeps me peaceful and without stress. The way I think and eat supports a healthy mind.

MY SPIRIT

To me, spirit determines one's character. It is expression, liveliness, and energy. Through my experience with meditation, I have learned there is also an inner spirit, which is physically intangible. This spirit connects us to a higher place and deeper realizations of the self. Our thoughts, words, and deeds come from our spirit. I believe our spirit is our real authentic self. Life lessons or karma—what we experience while on earth—is connected to our inner spirit.

10 steps for maintaining memory, mobility, independence, and beauty

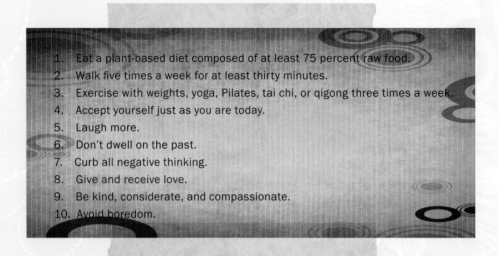

1. Eat a plant-based diet composed of at least 75 percent raw food.
2. Walk five times a week for at least thirty minutes.
3. Exercise with weights, yoga, Pilates, tai chi, or qigong three times a week.
4. Accept yourself just as you are today.
5. Laugh more.
6. Don't dwell on the past.
7. Curb all negative thinking.
8. Give and receive love.
9. Be kind, considerate, and compassionate.
10. Avoid boredom.

the pitfalls of what we eat right now

With age-related diseases showing up much earlier than in previous generations and obesity on the rise at an alarming rate, poor health and premature aging are universal topics. Our health and the food we eat are of major concern.

We use food to suppress and express emotions. We celebrate holidays and special occasions with food and drink and many times go overboard, throwing common sense out the window. Celebrating is fantastic as long as we don't abuse food and alcohol and find ourselves in a food coma or have too much to drink and need a ride home after a party.

Food is entertainment. We have business lunches, drown our sadness, and go through life using food for pleasure. We diet, starve, binge, and purge ourselves to look like models. Food is used in many ways to deal with life's ups and downs. When you learn to eat for health and not solely entertainment or because you are so hungry you would eat the first thing you see, you will be able to celebrate and thoroughly enjoy the right choice of foods for their nutritional value wherever you are.

By now, most health-conscious people know about the dangers of fats, sodium, and sugars in processed foods. We are aware of hormones, antibiotics, and tranquilizers being pumped into animals at factory farms and the inhumane treatment used in raising these animals. Diabetes, cancer, heart disease, osteoporosis, and a host of other illnesses are linked to eating animals. Millions try drugs, surgery, and fad diets hoping to improve their physical appearance only to find they look artificial and the results are short-term. But if we make simple, smart changes to our diet, we can live a long and healthy life and look ageless. It doesn't take a scientist to tell us that a handful of almonds are better for us than a handful of cookies or chips.

Even though many of us are concerned about our health, unhealthy eating habits are hard to break, especially in our fast-paced society where fast food is on every corner. What will it take for you to make healthier choices, and how do you know the choices you make will bring the results you are seeking? Reading this book is a good sign you are ready to make some positive changes.

In *Live Raw*, I hope to inspire you with substantial information on how making simple changes can produce remarkable results in your health, weight, appearance, and vitality. *Live Raw* provides a way to lose weight easily and naturally and keep it off without complicated calorie counting, measurements, or feelings of deprivation. You will learn a natural way to heal yourself without using medication and prescription. For those of you who feel insecure about aging, you will learn how to look better simply by adopting a healthy lifestyle and gaining self-love.

Secrets to good health are not complicated, and with Mother Nature's wisdom, you will learn to replace "bad-for-you foods" with "good-for-you foods" and unconscious eating with awareness. My book is based on a simple green-cuisine, plant-based diet, and I love providing some of my delicious recipes—proving taste does not have to be sacrificed while getting the benefits of healthy food. Anyone can prepare a green juice or smoothie in just a few minutes, which can change one's health habits in a dynamic and positive way forever. In addition to sharing my approach to life, I hope to change the current stereotype of aging.

Although my focus and philosophy is on making raw, plant-based food an everyday habit, vegetarians and non-vegetarians can pick and choose what works best for their lifestyle. For those looking to shed extra pounds, avoid or eliminate disease, feel more energetic, and add good years to life, *Live Raw* will provide many options. You don't have to sacrifice every indulgence, just the life-shortening ones, and as a result, you won't just stay alive longer, you will *live* longer, look better, be happier, and feel years younger. The only thing you will lose is what you are trying to get rid of, and what you will gain is what you have always wanted.

> **Change your thoughts, and you change your world.**
> —Norman Vincent Peale (1898–1993)

WHAT THE STANDARD AMERICAN DIET (SAD) HAS CREATED

We know that what we eat matters, but that doesn't make it any easier to change our diets and eat healthier.

Since we can't see what's going on inside our bodies, we take our time committing to healthier eating habits unless we get sick. Only when we start seeing those little pesky lines on our face, or weigh more than we'd like, or wake up with aches and pains, are we prepared to commit to a healthier lifestyle.

Science says we age faster as we grow older. Toxins build up, and our DNA breaks down over the years. As we age, we are exposed to the environment, stress, and bad eating habits for a longer period. Our body doesn't repair itself as quickly as it did in our earlier years, so it seems logical that we age at a faster rate.

We go along in our thirties and forties aging at a faster rate than in our twenties. Then we reach our fifties and start to notice more little signs like a line here and a little sag there, a pain here and a pain there, and all of a sudden, we notice we are aging faster. It is much easier in our thirties and forties to look younger than our actual age, but in our fifties it becomes more of a challenge. And because the rate of aging is exponential, in our sixties and seventies and beyond this, the process only accelerates.

I've seen the results of cosmetic fixes. After all, I grew up in Hollywood and worked in the film industry for eighteen years. Yo-yo dieting and diet pills play havoc on health. I saw how Botox froze expressive faces, how fake collagen lip injections can look, and how plastic surgery can go terribly wrong.

So the questions are, how fast or slow do we age, what causes the aging process, and how do we want to experience life in our later years? How can we age gracefully, be healthy, remain vital, and still look good?

Slowing down the degeneration of cells, bones, muscle, and connective tissue takes some know-how and a little work. I know it's difficult to adopt new routines and to break old habits, but if we wait too long to get started, the cell damage from free radicals will be harder to reverse and you might spend some time not feeling your best. It's not impossible to change things, and it's never too late to do something about the ravages of time even if you wait until middle age, but I suggest you might want to get down to business and start as soon as possible.

WHAT'S WRONG WITH THE FOOD WE EAT?

Let's see if you can recognize some foods you might eat that can make a difference in your health. Some unhealthy foods are quite obvious—including sugar, trans fats, dairy products, fried foods, junk foods, and sweetened carbonated drinks—which are just empty calories and void of nutrients. There is no room for these foods in a healthy diet. When we eat these types of foods, we tend to overeat and never feel quite satisfied. The fats, sugars, salt, and other ingredients contained in these foods make them addicting. Once you start, you can't stop, and before you know it, you've finished a bag of chips or a box of cookies in one sitting.

Consuming starches and food with gluten—which is part of the rubbery protein found in wheat, rye, barley oats, breads, pastries, cookies, cakes, biscuits, crackers, battered foods, pasta, pizza, snack foods—can make you feel tired minutes after you finish a meal. Many people of all ages are gluten intolerant and have what is known as celiac disease. It appears that the number of people with celiac disease is growing, and you will see many products on the shelves today that say "gluten free." Many health practitioners recommend a gluten-free and dairy-free diet for children with autism.

There are times when we eat a large meal and feel really full, but within an hour we are hungry again. These are all common situations, and many of us have felt this way at one time or another. Only you know how you feel after eating and drinking, and only you know if the food you consumed energized you or dragged you down.

The reason we feel sluggish, tired, and full but not satisfied after eating is that we are not getting enough of the nutrients from the food we consume. When eating processed or packaged foods, we are filling ourselves with low-nutrient food and chemicals. Our digestive system is working overtime to process these foods, which may stay in the body for days undigested.

When we eat foods that are unprocessed, uncooked, and in their natural state just as Mother Nature intended—including fruits, vegetables, nuts, seeds, and sprouts—we are eating foods that contain all the vitamins and nutrients our body requires to be healthy into our later years. These foods digest quickly, give our body the proper nutrients, and exit the body without taxing it.

DAIRY PRODUCTS

Animal protein of any kind is difficult to digest. Many years of study after study claim milk, cheese, and eggs contribute to heart diseases and the aging process. Because of their higher saturated fat content, increased skin inflammation, digestion problems, and faster aging of the cells have been found in those who consume dairy products. Many researchers, including Dr. William Ellis, a retired osteopathic physician and surgeon in Arlington, Texas, who researched the effects of dairy products for over forty-two years, say dairy products are simply no good for humans. Dr. Ellis is not alone in his belief that the excess mucus caused by milk can harden to form a coating along the inner wall of the intestines, hindering the absorption of nutrients and possibly leading to chronic fatigue, allergies, and emotional problems.

I could quote numerous doctors from around the world who, through years of research, believe dairy should not be consumed. I meet many people that tell me it's hard to give up cheese. That French brie or Italian burrata might taste great, but do you take into consideration what it is doing to your health and the health of cows? Cheese is made from milk. It is high in saturated fat; it raises your cholesterol levels and causes you to put on unwanted pounds.

If you are a vegetarian and don't eat animal flesh because of compassion and moral reasons, you might just want to take a closer look at the animal dairy products you *are* consuming. Factory farm dairy cows are impregnated time after time. Dairy cows are shot up with hormones and steroids and are only good to the dairy farmer until they can't produce any more milk. At that time, it's obvious what happens to them. Baby calves are taken from their mother as soon as they are born and do not have access to the lactating milk that is really meant for them, nor do they get their mother's nurturing all babies deserve and need. Many of the male calves are put into narrow wooden stalls so they can't move or turn around or even lie down comfortably. Veal is valued for its tenderness, and immobilizing and restricting the calves' movement leads to muscle deterioration. The baby calves are also fed an iron-deficient formula that forces them to be borderline anemic, and they suffer their whole very short life of eighteen to twenty months. As for the lactating milk, it is used for human consumption for drinking and making cheese.

An important ingredient in making conventional cheeses is the enzyme that comes from the lining of a calf's stomach and is called rennet. Calf rennet is extracted from the inner mucosa of the fourth stomach chamber (the abomasums) of young unweaned calves. The stomach is a by-product of veal production. In some cheese making, the stomach from pigs are used. Rennet is what causes the milk to coagulate and become cheese. A few years ago, it became common practice to mix the rennet from calf stomach with a pepsin enzyme that was derived from the stomachs of swine. This converts the milk into an almost solid mass, which makes it turn to cheese. There are some cheeses made without animal products and are a development of lactic acid. They are processed and taste fine, but they have no real value in an optimum healthy diet.

I know people who claim they do very well with raw cheese, but if you are eating for taste alone, you might want to consider if what you are eating is healthy for you and the animals. It's your decision, but for me, all animal products mean an animal was harmed in the process. I feel any pressure on animals, including forcing their milk production, has no place in a compassionate society.

Cheese lovers, don't fret. Just wait until you taste some of the nut cheese recipes and cheesecakes in this book. I think you will be quite surprised. They are easy to make, delicious, very eye appealing, and humane.

if I may take a moment to rant about animal consumption—please

For those of you who are not vegetarian or vegan, I suggest you just try cutting out animal consumption and products for a few days or for a few meals weekly. There is substantiating evidence that we can get all the nutrients we need from a plant-based diet. I know you think it might be hard to give up eating animals—you like the way meat tastes and you've been told you need the protein—but I guarantee you will feel and look years younger getting those animal toxins out of your body. Animal consumption is linked to colon cancer, breast cancer, prostate cancer, constipation, gout, high blood pressure, strokes, arthritis, obesity, and much more. Animals are injected with hormones, drugs, chemicals, and antibiotics. Many farmers use tranquilizers before killing the animal, and when you eat animals, you are ingesting all those drugs and all the fear from the animal. These tranquilizers are especially used on factory-farm animals, including pigs, lambs, goats, cattle, chickens, and turkeys.

Animal flesh takes lots of energy and digestive juices to break down in the stomach and usually takes days to digest once eaten. Humans do not have the proper stomach acid to digest animal flesh, and that is why it stays in the colon so long.

Here is an interesting theory: Meat-eating animals have claws, and herbivores do not. Meat-eating animals have strong hydrochloric acid in their stomachs, whereas human's stomach acid is twenty times weaker than meat-eating animals. A meat-eating animal's intestinal tract is only three times its body length, so decaying meat can pass through more quickly. Our intestinal tract is ten to twelve times our body length, giving meat time to decay. Even animals in the wild, with their proper teeth and stomach acids, need a long time to rest and recuperate in order to digest after eating their prey. If you think about it, when you take a bite of steak and chew it, in the first few chews you get the taste, and after that, you are chewing just to process and break down the meat to swallow after the taste is long gone.

Another reason to stop eating animals is the moral issue. It's the reason I became a vegetarian and then a vegan. Thousands of animals are killed every day in slaughterhouses. They are tortured, beaten, left to bleed to death, and fear for their lives just like we would in the same position. Compassion for all living beings can make a person feel very different in mind, body, and spirit. We must stop any kind of killing and torture in order to have peace on this planet, and this includes the brutal treatment of animals that are raised for food. To me, it is barbaric.

Millions of tons of grain and water are fed to livestock, while millions of people around the world are starving and being denied clean water. There is pollution from factory farms, including massive groundwater problems. Animal consumption is at an all-time high and has quadrupled in the last fifty years. Billions of livestock are taking up space on our earth, more than triple that of humans. We are chopping down rain forests to make room for raising cattle. Worldwatch Institute claims that global livestock population has risen 60 percent since 1961. Aside from population expansion, much of this growth has to do with fast-food restaurants, whose food is making Americans overweight and sick.

The Department of Health and Human Services states in a recent report that children today will not live as long as their parents. The reason given is obesity. This is a shocking statistic. The author of *Fast Food Nation*, Eric Schlosser, says, "Americans now spend more money on fast food—$110 billion a year—than they do on higher education." We spend more on fast food than on movies, books, magazines, newspapers, videos, and recorded music—combined.

You might have heard all this information before, or you might not be ready to hear it yet, but it's true and important to know. Whether you stop eating animals for your health or stop because of your compassion for animals (worldwide, some 56 billion animals are raised and slaughtered for food each year), or if you stop for concerns about the environment and our planet, you must stop soon.

You can take time to transition into a plant-based diet. You can add more greens slowly, you can even cook your vegetables, but the issue of eating animals is one that is vital to how all our lives around the world are to be lived in the coming decades. It affects all of us. Please educate yourself on the subject and make the compassionate choice.

Cashew Parmesan Cheese

CHAPTER 2

WHAT
to eat and
WHY

function of major body parts

As the caretaker of your body, you will need to know how to keep these parts working at optimum health and peak performance. To make it easy for yourself to get these necessary vitamins and minerals, I'm going to tell you exactly what they are and how you can get them from a plant-based diet. I'm going to show you how to be completely nourished, healthy, and compassionate without animals being harmed in the process.

BRAIN: We use this organ to reason, think, and make decisions. Alzheimer and dementia take all that away.
  What Is Needed: Omega-3 and good fats
  Foods to Eat: Flaxseed, walnuts, apples, red grapes, blueberries, spinach, cranberries, strawberries, avocados

EYES: We use them to see everything we do, along with the faces of our loved ones, a flower, the sky, mountains, oceans, trees, and all the beauty there is in the world. If we don't take care of our eyes, we can get macular degeneration, eye diseases, and lose our sight.
  What Is Needed: Vitamin A, lutein, beta-carotene, antioxidants
  Foods to Eat: Spinach, broccoli, carrots, cantaloupe, sweet potatoes, pumpkin, red bell pepper, dark greens, berries, red grapes, garlic

HEART: Allows us to lead a healthy, active lifestyle and do the things we love. High blood pressure and high cholesterol can shorten our lives.
  What Is Needed: Folate, potassium, alpha-carotene, fiber
  Foods to Eat: Bananas, berries, spinach, broccoli, tomatoes, oranges, dark leafy greens, carrots, pumpkin seeds, oats, peas, watermelon, sprouts, pomegranate

BONES: Living tissue that needs attention. We may get osteoporosis and not be able to participate in daily activities. We can break a hip easily, and with bad bones, we may walk hunched over with canes and walkers as we age.
  What Is Needed: Vitamin D, calcium, magnesium, bromelain
  Foods to Eat: Pineapple, arugula, broccoli, dark leafy greens, cherries, button mushrooms, almonds, spinach, and sunshine

SKIN, HAIR, AND NAILS: We all want to look good as we age. Skin and hair are two things that we judge our looks and health on. Wrinkles and hair loss are not something we look forward to.
  What Is Needed: Vitamins A, C, and E
  Foods to Eat: Spinach, carrots, chard, sweet potatoes, tomatoes, cantaloupe, squash, cabbage, pineapples, oranges, kiwis, red and yellow bell peppers, broccoli, almonds, seeds, papaya, cucumber, walnuts

MUSCLES: We need them for stability and balance. Skeletal muscles are responsible for all our voluntary movements. Without muscle tone, the body is weak and susceptible to injury. A gym is not necessary for optimum muscle health, and much can be done in the privacy of your own home.
  What Is Needed: Protein, omega-3, chromium
  Foods to Eat: Walnuts, sprouts, flaxseed, chia seeds, hemp seeds, green peppers, apples, bananas, spinach

TEETH AND GUMS: We don't want to lose our teeth, not only because we don't want to put our false ones in a glass of water at night, but also because they have a lot to do with the overall health of our internal system. When you have dental problems, you can be assured that other health problems will show up; bacteria of the mouth are warning signs. My father used to say, "Without good gums, there are no teeth; without teeth, there is no chewing; without chewing, there is no life."

What Is Needed: Vitamins A, C, and D

Foods to Eat: Broccoli, tomato, papaya, mango, jicama, kiwi, carrots, pumpkin, cantaloupe, dark green leafy vegetables, exposure to sun for vitamin D, or supplements may be advised

LIVER: Reports claim over 30 million Americans suffer from liver disease. Fifty to seventy-five percent are nonalcoholic fatty liver disease caused by obesity diabetes. A healthy liver is necessary to keep toxins out of our bloodstream. Our vitality depends upon having a healthy liver. The liver controls virtually every internal activity. If the liver is impaired, it can impair other body functions.

What Is Needed: Herbal supplements: milk thistle, fennel seed, dandelion root, turmeric. Avoid hydrogenated fats, trans fats, saturated fats, alcohol, sugar, artificial sweeteners, white flour, and caffeine.

Foods to Eat: Beets, apples, artichokes, blueberries, radishes, arugula, fruits, dark leafy greens

KIDNEY: The arteries bring blood and waste into our kidneys, then the kidney cleans the blood and releases the extra fluid through the urine, leaving clean blood to go through the kidneys and back into the bloodstream through the veins. It is very important that this system works at its best, including avoiding substances that damage the liver.

What Is Needed: Vitamins B_6, D, E, and C

Foods to Eat: Broccoli, turnips, spinach, celery, nuts, high-water-content fruits such as oranges, berries, grapes, watermelon

GALLBLADDER: This tiny organ below the liver and rib cage is shaped like a little eggplant and helps the liver process fats. The gallbladder works along with your liver to keep bile from piling up. The production and flow of the bile decreases with aging. As a result, gallstones are more likely to form. Gallstones often arise from high fat intake. Generally, people who are overweight and have high cholesterol are more prone to gallbladder problems. If we want to keep all our body parts healthy, even the ones we can't see, diet is the key.

What Is Needed: Avoid carbonated drinks, fatty and fried foods; drink at least six glasses of water daily

Foods to Eat: Olive oil, flaxseed and flaxseed oil, beets and beet greens, cabbage, broccoli, sprouts, all berries, sweet potato, butternut squash, carrots, fruits high in water content

grocery list

Nuts and seeds—almonds, brazil nuts, walnuts, pecans, sunflower seeds, pumpkin seeds, hemp seeds, chia seeds, flaxseeds.

Fruits and berries—oranges, apples, pineapple, kiwis, watermelons, bananas, cantaloupes, blackberries, raspberries, blueberries, grapes, grapefruit, cranberries, strawberries, avocados, tomatoes, pears, peaches, nectarines, apricots, pomegranates.

Vegetables—spinach, kale, collard, romaine, parsley, cilantro, arugula, green peas, sweet potatoes, carrots, pumpkin, broccoli, brussels sprouts, watercress, red/yellow/green bell peppers, mushrooms, butternut squash.

DRINK YOUR FRUITS AND VEGETABLES!

Looking at the chart of what foods we need to nourish our body, you may begin to have some idea of the many varieties of foods we need to consume daily to keep our body healthy. I suggest juicing or making smoothies as it would be difficult to consume large quantities of fruits and vegetables if you were chewing them. Each body is different, but if you can drink one or two quarts of juice or smoothie a day, which include a variety of fruits and vegetables, you can be comfortable knowing you are giving your cells many of the vitamins and nutrients they need.

I know many of you don't have time to cut, chop, and peel, but when organized, most of these drinks take ten minutes or less to prepare. If you purchase juices or smoothies at a health food store or juice bar, make sure it's fresh squeezed. Bottled juices are processed and oxidize quickly, losing much of their nutritional value. If a juice is not squeezed in front of you, be sure to check ingredients at smoothie and juice bars, as many have added sugars, are concentrated, and are not as healthy as they appear to be.

A smoothie can be made quickly and include any fruits and vegetables you enjoy and contain a boost of vitamins you might want to increase. A high-powered blender will make your drink smooth, creamy, and extra delicious. All you do is place rough chopped fruit and greens with filtered water into a blender and turn on the motor. Drink it down or pour it in a container or thermos, and off you go. You will get your antioxidants, boost your immunity, and give your cells all they need to function at their highest level.

When juicing, don't worry about losing fiber; this predigested drink will give you a complete value of nutrients. I personally juice more than I make smoothies. Many days I do both: I juice, then pour into my blender, add berries, mango, or other fruit, and blend. The important thing is to drink your daily green drink. You can use the pulp for soups and vegetable patties or just compost.

detoxifying—so gravity won't get you down

Here is a simple three-to-five-day detoxifying program to get you started. I know you can do anything for three to five days—right? You may eat any of the dishes here—in any order and as much as you like.

WHAT TO EXPECT

1. You will be consuming fruits, vegetables, smoothies, juices, soups, and salads. Make a list of the fruits and vegetables you will need to shop for and buy organic, as you don't want to consume pesticides and chemicals, especially during this detox.
2. You will not be consuming bread, meat, fish, dairy, alcohol, processed foods, refined sugars, fats, oils, avocado, nuts, seeds, dried fruit, coffee, or alcohol.
3. For dinner the night before officially starting your detox, eat as much fruit as you like and drink as much water as you like.

4. If you feel hungry during the detox, eat more as long as the food is allowed on the program; don't go hungry.

5. Drink a glass of lemon water upon arising with juice from one lemon and one or more cups water.

6. You may eat any of the recipes in any order and any time of the day.

7. If you have craving for food on the "you can't have" list, forget it. It's only a few days, and you can live without it. Nibble some veggies or fruit, and drink water.

8. Good detox foods to add to drink, soups, and salad are the following: broccoli or pea sprouts, lemon, dark leafy greens, watercress, garlic, and ginger.

When you complete the detox, continue to eat light for a day or so. Try to have a smoothie daily, and check out some of the lighter raw food recipes in the book. Think before you eat something and ask yourself if it will promote better health. Just being more conscious about what you put in your mouth will make a difference.

TIP {
Peel bananas that have dark speckle spots on them and freeze in ziplock bag to add to smoothies.

Cut and freeze any seasonal fruit to use in smoothies to create a slushy cold drink.

Juice greens, celery, cucumber, and apples and add to blender with fruit of your choice.

Remember to add water to make the consistency you prefer—thick or thin, you choose. Blending in a generous amount of ice gives drinks a nice frosty taste and texture.
}

Recipes for Detox Smoothies and Salads

BANANA SMOOTHIE

2 bananas

4 stalks of celery

1 apple, cut in quarters

3 handfuls of spinach

½ cucumber, cut in half

1½ cups of filtered water or to your liking

Add ice and blend in high-speed blender.

ORANGE SMOOTHIE

2 oranges, peeled and cut in quarters

7 kale leaves, stems removed

1½ cups water or to your liking

1 green apple, cut in quarters

Handful of berries

Add ice and blend in high-speed blender.

PINEAPPLE SMOOTHIE

1 cup pineapple

1 pint of berries

3 handfuls of your favorite dark greens

1 to 1½ cups water or to your liking

Add ice and blend in high-speed blender.

PEACH SMOOTHIE

2 frozen bananas

7 kale leaves, stems removed

Water as needed to arrive at a consistency you like

2 peaches, cut in quarters

1 handful of sprouts

Add ice and blend in high-speed blender.

PEAR SMOOTHIE

2 pears, cut in quarters

1 frozen banana

Water as needed to arrive at a consistency you like

2 apples, cut in quarters

1 sprig of mint

Add ice and blend in high-speed blender.

EXTRA DRINK TREATS

Blend 3 cups of watermelon with water, ice, and a pinch of salt

Blend 3 cups cantaloupe with water and ice

Blend 3 cups pineapple with water and ice

soups

You can eat soups warm or cold. To warm, place soup in a pan on the stove, stirring continually to warm slightly. Do not overheat in order to retain nutrients. Dry or fresh herbs and light spices may be added to soups.

TOMATO SOUP

3 tomatoes, cut in quarters

½ red bell pepper

¼ cup sweet onion

5 basil leaves

Juice from 1 lime

Water as needed to arrive at a consistency you like (a little chunky is good)

⅓ cup sun-dried tomatoes, soaked until soft

½ cucumber

1 clove garlic

Pinch of chili flakes

Pinch of salt

Blend in high-speed blender. May be warmed.

BROCCOLI SOUP

½ cup broccoli

1 handful spinach

Water as needed to arrive at a consistency you like

½ red bell pepper

2 kale leaves, stems removed

Blend in high-speed blender. May be warmed.

CHILLED CUCUMBER SOUP

1 cucumber, chopped in thirds

¼ piece of onion

Pinch of salt

1 rib of celery, cut in chunks

1 tablespoon dill

Water as needed to arrive at a consistency you like

Blend in high-speed blender.

SPINACH SOUP

2 handfuls spinach

1 rib of celery

Juice from ½ lemon

Water as needed to arrive at a consistency you like

½ red bell pepper

½ clove garlic

Herbs, including cumin, turmeric, coriander

Blend in high-speed blender.

GREEN SOUP

1 cucumber

1 scallion

½ cup alfalfa sprouts

Water as needed to arrive at a consistency you like

5 leaves of kale, stems removed

2 handfuls spinach or romaine lettuce

2 tomatoes, cut into quarters

Blend in high-speed blender.

salads

I could just about live on salads alone. Although these detox salads do not have the usual dressing, I find them refreshing and light. Find a nice large bowl and fill it up. You will soon be craving more greens.

 TIP { Any salad mix can be rolled in a lettuce leaf for a change of pace. Butter lettuce, romaine, and chard leaves work well and roll easily. A raw nori sheet is also acceptable.
Use most any salad from the salad section of the book, eliminating the dressings.
Feel free to add more veggies you like to any salad.

ARUGULA BROCCOLI SALAD

¼ cup red onion, diced

1 cup arugula

½ cup jicama, julienned

1 cup broccoli, small bud

¼ cup corn kernels

Dressing

3 tablespoons lemon or lime juice

Pinch of salt

Water if necessary

2 cloves garlic, minced

Dash of cayenne

BEET SALAD

1 cup beets, shredded

Dressing

Use juice from one apple and a dash of apple cider vinegar. This dressing is also delicious with sliced cucumbers.

CHOPPED TOMATOES WITH CILANTRO

1 cup chopped tomatoes

1 tablespoon dill

1 bunch cilantro, chopped

Juice from ½ lime

VEGGIE SALAD

Use equal amounts of each vegetable: yellow squash, zucchini, asparagus, broccoli, string beans, turnip, and baby lettuce greens.

All ingredients should be chopped very, very small.

Dressing

Mint

Dill

Lemon juice

MIXED DARK GREEN SALAD

1 romaine, chopped into ribbon-cut pieces

3 collard leaves, stems removed and ribbon cut

½ cup cucumbers, chopped

½ cup mushrooms, chopped

½ cup red bell pepper, chopped

6 leaves kale, stems removed and ribbon cut

2 handfuls spinach, ribbon cut

¼ cup red onion, chopped

½ cup parsley leaves, chopped

Dressing

Juice of 1 orange

1 teaspoon dill

more dressings

CUCUMBER DRESSING

½ cucumber

1 tablespoon dill

1 scallion

Pinch of salt

Place in blender and blend until smooth.

JUST LEMON DRESSING

If you can find Myers lemons at your market, they are sweet enough to squeeze directly on a salad. A few fresh herbs and that's all you need. A regular lemon is fine, but not as sweet.

APPLE CIDER VINEGAR

Touch of apple cider vinegar

Touch of apple juice to sweeten

Juice of 1 orange

29 Tips for Staying Young at Any Age

It's true that what we eat plays a major role in our health. But our attitude, outlook, and a few simple lifestyle tips will contribute to a long, happy, and healthy life.

1. DON'T MESS WITH MOTHER NATURE

A key component to good health is organic, live, plant-based foods. Those of us who eat raw food refer to our food as "live" because the enzymes in fresh fruits and vegetables are still alive as opposed to processed or cooked foods. Live foods include organic, locally grown fruits, vegetables, sprouts, nuts, and seeds uncooked and unprocessed, out of the ground or off the tree, and eaten as close to their natural state as possible.

Research shows that cooking food depletes vitamins, oxidizes them, and destroys enzymes. A raw, plant-based diet benefits digestion and body functions because the enzymes stay intact. When you eat foods that lack the necessary nutrients your body requires on a daily basis, you tend to overeat because your body is not satisfied.

Because much of our produce is genetically modified and our fruits and vegetables are picked early to leave time for shipping to market, nutrients and antioxidants in mass-produced, conventional commercial produce are declining. We purchase fruit that will never ripen properly or give us their full nutritional value or taste. You might have noticed the fruit and vegetables we buy today at our conventional markets certainly don't taste as good as they used to. The difference in vegetables fresh from the garden, or heirloom breeds (not genetically altered), is significant. Peaches used to drip with sweet nectar, apples were crisp and juicy, and fruit would ripen properly. You may have noticed that quite often, fruit from today's supermarkets will rot shortly after purchase or, in some cases, not ripen at all.

Organic produce is proven to contain more nutrients than conventionally grown produce. Pesticides in conventional foods are known to contribute to or cause serious illnesses. Each year, the Environmental Working Group, a nonprofit organization dedicated to protecting public health and the environment, provides a list called the "Dirty Dozen," which includes a list of the most chemically treated fruits and vegetables. Research found that those who eat the twelve most contaminated fruits and vegetables consume an average of ten pesticides a day, while those who eat the fifteen least-contaminated conventionally grown fruits and vegetables ingest fewer than two pesticides daily.

Children are the most sensitive to pesticide intake. The following is a list of the "Dirty Dozen." Print this information on a card and carry it in your wallet or purse as a reminder when grocery shopping.

"The Dirty Dozen"— Foods Best *NOT* to Consume Unless They Are Organically Grown:

Fruits
Apples, cherries, grapes, nectarines, peaches, pears, strawberries
Vegetables
Bell peppers, carrots, celery, lettuce

Though these are not on the targeted list, I would add all root vegetables as well. The most common are beets, burdock, carrots, celeriac, turnips, parsnip, potatoes, sweet potatoes, and radishes.

If you do buy conventionally grown produce, these are the foods that contain lower amounts of pesticides:

Fruits
Avocado, kiwi, mango, tomato, papaya, pineapple, watermelon
Vegetables
Asparagus, broccoli, corn, cabbage, eggplant, onion, sweet peas

The reason I still prefer to buy all organic is because of troubling studies done on a range of twenty-five antioxidant-rich foods, including broccoli, tomatoes, bananas, apples, onions, and others. Of these foods, those not grown organically showed a loss of 57% of vitamin C and iron, 28% of calcium, 100% loss of vitamin A, 50% loss of riboflavin, and an 18% loss of thiamine. Of these seven nutrients analyzed, only the levels of niacin increased in nonorganic produce versus the organic produce. When I eat, I always want the best nutritional value in the food I consume, and organic surpasses nonorganic.

You deserve the very best, so don't skimp on buying yourself the finest fresh organic foods possible. You might spend money on material things like clothes or jewelry, but if you don't put the same attention into maintaining your body, you will pay for it in the long run. Your health is the most valuable possession you own and your body is the only one you have, so treat it well.

Organic produce picked at peak timing, brought to a farmers' market, and consumed shortly afterward is the best way to know you are getting the most from what you eat, in taste and in vitamins. When you choose to buy organic, you spend less money in the long run, as you tend to eat less because you are getting all your nutrients and feel more nourished. Medical bills may be reduced, and money spent on drugs and supplements can be eliminated. You might spend a little more in the long run because you will live a longer life—but I think the life you live will be worth the price.

2. ANTIOXIDANTS—STOPPING FREE RADICALS IN THEIR TRACKS

This is the only technical portion of the book, but it's very important to understand, so I will make this as simple as possible. Most of us have heard the term "free radicals." Free radicals are molecules. A molecule is defined as an electrically neutral group of at least two atoms in a definite arrangement held together by very strong chemical bonds. This is as technical as I plan to get. In short, free radicals are unstable and dangerous and are responsible for aging and damaging our tissues. Free radicals roam our body, looking to bond with other molecules that might be stable. Free radicals destroy the vitality of stable molecules. They are responsible for clogged arteries, and studies have proven they can cause heart disease and strokes. Free radicals accumulate with age.

Here's how they work: once the free radical damages a stable molecule, that molecule then becomes a free radical (sounds a little like *Dracula*). It works like a chain reaction in our body.

The free radical's enemy—drumroll please—is the antioxidant. Antioxidants are found in vegetables and fruits, especially in beta-carotene, vitamin C, A, and E. These vitamins are the defenders. They protect the stable molecules from the roaming free radicals.

How many times have you heard "Eat your fruits and vegetables"? Well, it's true. Fresh fruits and vegetables are the best way to get the vitamins and minerals you need for a healthy body. They are more powerful than taking supplements because the body can absorb and process them better. You can overdo vitamins, and long-term use of supplements has not been proven effective and can even be harmful to your liver. The following is a list of foods naturally high in antioxidants:

Fruits–blackberries, blueberries, cherries, cranberries, strawberries, raspberries, pomegranates, grapes, oranges, plums, pineapples, kiwis, prunes, dates, apricots, lemons, apples, and grapefruits.

Vegetables–kale, red cabbage, carrots, peppers, parsley, artichokes, brussels sprouts, spinach, and red beets.

Nuts and Seeds–pecans, walnuts, hazelnuts, sunflower seeds, pumpkin seeds, chia seeds, and hemp seeds.

Spices–ginger, chili pepper, cloves, cinnamon, cumin, turmeric, and oregano.

To reap the most benefits from antioxidant-rich foods and to absorb all their nutrients, consume them in their natural raw state. For example, fresh wild blueberries provide a huge amount of antioxidants if you eat them raw, but you will lose much of the nutritional value by cooking them in a pie (not to mention the added sugar).

3. THERE'S A POT OF GOLD AT THE END OF THE RAINBOW

Your body will get all the nutrients it needs from a colorful array of fruits and vegetables. The following color chart will tell you what foods will help keep your body strong and healthy.

Red fruits

Red fruits are colored by natural plant pigments called lycopene and anthocyanin and contain phytochemical, which are natural disease fighters. Look for these red fruits and vegetables: red apples, strawberries, cranberries, raspberries, tomatoes, red cabbage, red peppers, beets, red grapes, watermelon, cherries, and pomegranates. They help reduce, reverse, and prevent diseases including diabetes, heart disease, strokes, hypertension, and high cholesterol. They reduce the risk of a variety of cancers, including those of the lung, prostate, ovaries, and cervix. They are also known to improve brain function. Red fruits and vegetables are full of antioxidants, minerals, and vitamins including magnesium, calcium, zinc, and potassium, fiber, folate, and vitamins C and A.

Orange and yellow produce

Orange and yellow produce are loaded with carotenoids and are high in vitamin C. Sweet potatoes and carrots contain loads of potassium. Beta-carotene, which is found in foods such as carrots, sweet potatoes, cantaloupe, and winter squash, is converted to vitamin A, which helps your skin and vision. When you consume pumpkins, carrots, apricots, oranges, peaches, yellow apples, mangoes, papaya, pears, and pineapple, you are giving your body magnesium and calcium that help keep your bones strong.

Dark green leafy vegetables

Dark green leafy vegetables get their color from chlorophyll and are full of fiber, vitamins, minerals, and phytochemicals. Dark green leafy vegetables such as kale, collard greens, romaine lettuce, cilantro, parsley, cabbage, broccoli, green beans, cucumbers, peas, zucchini, green pepper, and spinach all contain vitamin B and C, which help your body make protein. They are rich in fiber, folic acid, and lutein. Green vegetables and fruits contain natural antioxidants and help control bad cholesterol. Greens aid in digestion and can improve the immune system. Green vegetables are a source of iron and calcium, and can be sweet, bitter, or peppery tasting. Choose any greens you like for your salad or juice and you can't go wrong. They are low in fat and high in dietary fiber.

Blue and purple fruits

These fruits are deeply colored, thanks to natural plant pigments called anthocyanins that are high in powerful antioxidants: blackberries, blueberries, plums, raisins, purple grapes, purple cabbage, and figs. These fruits help prevent heart disease and promote healthy aging and strong eyes. They regulate digestion and protect the urinary tract from infection. They also restore antioxidant levels and reverse age-related brain decline.

4. AN APPLE A DAY KEEPS THE DOCTOR AWAY

Because of the pectin contained in apples, they are considered good for the heart.

They are known for decreasing cholesterol levels and preventing colon cancer. The pectin in apples can help clean out our intestines, so when you need a quick snack, grab an apple or two.

My other favorite apple is the old-time remedy—apple cider vinegar. I've been convinced for years that it cures many ailments including colds, allergies, flu, candida, acid reflux, sore throats, arthritis, and high blood pressure to name a few. You might think you wouldn't like the taste, and maybe at first you won't, but if you get past the thought and try it a few times, you will not mind it at all.

Here's how I drink it: two tablespoons in one cup of water, or if too strong, add more water. Drink this in the morning or anytime throughout

the day. Once a day is sufficient unless you are coming down with a cold, then twice a day is advisable. I've used it for years, and still think it's one of the best remedies around. It alkalizes the body and brings a healthy glow to your complexion.

I use apple cider vinegar in many of my salad dressing recipes and I've even use apple cider vinegar diluted with water to clean my kitchen surfaces, windows, and garbage cans. Pour a little down your garbage disposal to eliminate odors.

5. READ FOOD LABELS BEFORE YOU BUY ANY PRODUCT

If you can't pronounce it, don't eat it! Most processed foods are filled with additives and stripped of nutrients. They are full of sweeteners, fats, colorings, and preservatives. If an ingredient is difficult to pronounce or if there are a long list of ingredients, walk away from that product.

As strange as the following ingredients may seem, they are actually found in food products. These items are a big NO-NO, so don't buy products that list any of the following: artificial butter, artificial color, sodium benzoate (benzene), high-fructose corn syrup, artificial sweeteners (except for Stevia or erythritol), trans fats, refined grains, high salt content, ammonium sulfate (fertilizer found in bread dough), carminic acid (dried and crushed insects used as a food dye), shellac (secretions of the female lac beetle to make shiny coating on candies), castoreum (anal glands of a beaver to enhance the flavor of raspberry candies and sweets), gum base (sheep secretion), L-cystine or cystine (human hair or duck feathers), Allura Red AC (coal tar used in red-colored candies, sodas, and other sweets), rennet (calf stomach to make cheeses), and silicon dioxide (sand used as an anti-caking agent) just to name a few. This list is one more reason to eat a plant-based diet.

6. MICROWAVE OVENS CONTAIN ELECTROMAGNETIC MAGNETIC FIELDS (EMFS)—DON'T USE THEM

Certainly don't stand by one when it's on, no matter how safe they tell you they are. Microwave ovens have been known to leak electromagnetic radiation, and when tested with a Gauss meter (an instrument that measures the strength of magnetic fields), they were shown to emit radiation levels up to six feet away. Recently, one of my sons demonstrated this fact by using his meter to show us how far back we would need to stand from the microwave in order not to pick up any radiation when it is used. We were just about out the kitchen door.

Old or faulty door seals are the most common causes of microwave radiation leakage. Slamming the door, a buildup of dirt, or wear and tear can cause door seals to be less effective. It is advised by the FDA to not stand directly in front or close to a microwave oven while it is operating.

Microwave ovens are standard equipment in most kitchens. They are commonly used for heating up leftovers, popping popcorn, heating water, a cup of hot chocolate, or coffee, and cooking a full meal. They are used to make life fast and easy and more energy efficient. They work by creating high-frequency electromagnetic waves that penetrate food, causing its molecules to vibrate and generate heat within the food to cook it very quickly. They are considered a great time saver. You can have popcorn in minutes but please don't, as chemicals in the bag lining along with the butter flavoring leach into your popcorn, and these chemicals can accumulate in your body for years and eventually cause cancer. There are many good popcorn makers on the market. I suggest you buy one for your family to use and throw those microwave bags in the garbage.

Microwaves can convert food into dangerous toxic and carcinogenic products. There is a significant decrease in food value when food is cooked in a microwave oven and the cell wall of the food is destroyed, which can create free radicals. The body gets little or no benefit from food prepared in a microwave oven.

Break the habit and use your oven or stovetop, or better yet, eat raw and living foods.

Studies show that children are more susceptible to exposure from EMFs, so don't take chances.

7. WATER, WATER, AND MORE WATER

In my experience, eight to ten glasses of water per day is ideal. Plainly said, without water our skin will look like a prune. We need to hydrate, lubricate, and feed our cells and skin. The sun, environment, and stress dry us up inside and out. Hydrating will make our skin look younger. Don't get dehydrated; it plays havoc on many parts of our body's cells and can cause illness.

Don't wait until you are thirsty to drink water; it's usually a sign of dehydration. Because of the high water content in fruits and vegetables, a raw food diet helps keep you hydrated, but if you really want to know if you are hydrated, check the color of your urine. If your urine is dark or yellow, then you aren't drinking enough water. If your urine is clear, then you know you're getting enough water. Usually in the mornings our urine is darker, and throughout the day it becomes clearer. That's because during the night, we sweat and do not replace the lost water.

If you don't like plain water, add a squeeze of lemon, lime, or slice of cucumber to flavor the water.

To alkalinize an acidic body, which most of us have, first thing in the morning squeeze half a lemon in a cup of water and drink it down. You might also try my earlier suggestion of two tablespoons of apple cider vinegar in one cup of water. It's best not to drink water with a meal, as food should digest on its own. Drink thirty minutes before a meal or an hour after eating.

Now, what kind of water? Water, water everywhere and not a drop to drink. Well, almost any water is better than none at all, but there are lots of theories on this subject. Municipal tap water has been processed and treated. It could and usually does contain chlorine and fluoride. Chlorine in our water has been linked to cancer. Distilled water has no minerals and we need minerals. Bottled water could leach toxins from the plastic, and now we've been told that some big-name companies fill their bottles with water that is just purified municipal water. So what is the best drinking water?

We want water containing essential minerals and nutrients—like potassium and magnesium, found in water that comes from a well; natural springwater bottled at the source; or artesian possibly bottled and purified at a plant. Mineral waters come from underground sources and could contain the needed natural minerals.

Not everyone is going out to look for a spring to fill their bottles, but there are home filters that work very well, and any filter is better than no filter at all. I use a home filtration reverse osmosis alkalizing water system, and because it tastes so good, I find I enjoy drinking more water more often. I researched extensively before deciding on one and also tested all my friends' filtration systems. There are many good ones on the market, so do your research to find the best in your area. New systems are coming on the market constantly and with great improvements. Depending on your budget, there are filtration systems that sit on your kitchen countertop, ones that fit under your sink, and whole-house units that ensure filtered showers and baths.

Ozone is oxygen and ozonated water, which is made up of oxygen atoms, kills germs and bacteria but does not change the mineral content. Plastic pitchers with a filter on top will clean your water of chlorine, but in the process may also remove the minerals. Water is important for optimum heath, so it's worth the homework to find the best one. If there is a fountain of youth, you know that the water is flowing there freely.

Treat water as a precious commodity. The World Bank reports that eighty countries have water shortages and more than 2 billion people have no access to clean water or water sanitation.

8. STRESS

Stress can affect us mentally and physically. It releases chemicals into the blood and can age us prematurely. We can experience many forms of stress. If you are in danger or feel fearful, this is known as a fight-or-flight type of stress. This form of stress could help you react quickly in a hazardous situation. Self-inflicted stress could be caused by worrying about things we can't change. Stress can come from feeling rushed and never having enough time. Stress can come from work or personal relationships, school, or a business presentation. When we are stressed, it causes us to be more susceptible to sickness and disease and can leave us feeling depressed and fatigued. There are countless health problems that arise from stress, especially long-term stress.

Can we change from a high-stress person to a low-stress person? Can we take control and manage our stress? It could be time to simplify life and not overcommit to things that we really don't want or need to do. Stress is actually a sign of problems or conflicts that trouble us. Some stressful problems we experience seem not to be our fault. The economy, loss of jobs, and even loss of health make us feel stressed. Once labeled "stress," it becomes a problem bigger than life.

If we could refer to this so-called problem as a "challenge" instead of feeling stressed, we could then deal with it more effectively. The word *challenge* is defined as "a test of one's abilities or resources in a demanding but stimulating undertaking." We might see that stress is sometimes a self-inflicted state of mind and the challenge would be how to change this mental state. If financial stress affects us, we can take responsibility by looking at our previous spending habits and start correcting them; taking action helps relieve stress. If a stressful situation exists, calmly ask yourself what can be done to correct the situation. It's best to look for a solution to a challenge rather than feed the problem.

Having a spiritual or religious connection can help us deal with stress. Faith is a definite coping mechanism and a way to remind us things will work out and sometimes are even meant to be. Challenges come and go, and sometimes life seems good and sometimes not so good. This is the ebb and tide of living. Remember that the effects of stress can age you and can affect your mind and body just like anger and resentment. When you are seeking optimum health and longevity, you will find you have no room for these feelings.

Get organized, simplify your life, stop doing things you really don't want to do, and do more of the things you enjoy doing. Stop overspending and living a life you really can't afford. Start enjoying your health, your family, and your friends. Tell yourself the truth about what's bothering you, and make the necessary changes.

I can tell you from years of experience and challenges, issues you are stressed about today will be forgotten in the scope of your lifetime. Stay in the present and don't get attached to a problem. Leave room for the good things and quickly move through challenges and things that don't allow you to feel happy. Keep your health in mind and treat yourself kindly. Remember, "This too shall pass."

9. LOSE WEIGHT AND KEEP IT OFF

My doctor told me to stop having intimate dinners for four, unless there are three other people.

—Orson Welles

It's possible to lose weight without counting calories, weighing food, or getting on a scale. I'm proof.

There are lots of diets that help people lose weight, but not many of these diets take into consideration the health aspects of what they suggest we eat. Some diets have us eating processed foods filled with synthetic ingredients. Every day we read about companies who manufacture what they call "natural" and "low fat" foods. Many of these companies are now being cited for serious food safety violations. Some of the foods that claimed to be low fat are not low fat at all, and many are just chemical time bombs.

Many diets can help you take off weight, but they are not sustainable in the long term and end up failing. After the weight is lost, many of us go back to our usual way of eating and the pounds come back. No one wants to weigh, measure, and look at the calories in everything we eat for the rest of our lives. When we cut back on calories, we lower our metabolism and start to burn fewer calories, hence the diet stops working for us.

Some diets speed up our metabolism, putting undue strain on our bodies. Most weight-loss diets make us feel deprived and can cause guilt and low self-esteem. Just the word "diet" can make us feel we're not okay the way we are. I prefer to use the term "I'm eating for health."

How can we lose weight and make it a positive experience? When we make choices to eat for health and not for weight loss, we feel empowered instead of embarrassed. Eating for health is a form of self-love and not self-loathing.

Not everyone is built the same and not everyone will look like the models we see in magazines no matter how much weight is lost. What we must remember, even though we want to look good, is we need to feel good and be healthy. We've been told that eating less and exercising more will take the weight off. This might be true, but how many times have we done just that and then couldn't maintain the practice? We continue to lose the same twenty pounds over and over again.

Those who choose a raw food, plant-based lifestyle find that weight comes off quickly, easily, and naturally. You can only know if what I say is true by giving it a try and seeing the results for yourself. On page 18 you will find a detoxifying plan. Grab a friend or family member and partner up for an exciting health experience that will change the way you feel and look.

10. GET A GOOD NIGHT'S SLEEP

It still surprises me how many people don't get a good night's sleep. Friends of mine who eat raw food say they don't need as much sleep, but not me. I think sleep is important to maintaining a youthful look. I love my beauty sleep. Eight to nine hours is what I like best. It's true you can sleep less some nights, but it's not good for an extended practice. Lack of sleep leads to many health problems, along with grouchiness, lethargy, and wrinkles. Need I say more? Get some sleep!

Turn off the TV. Shut down your computer. Get a great pillow. Make sure you don't have a heavy meal close to your bedtime and avoid caffeine at night. If you can't sleep because you have too much on your mind, try to train yourself to let go of what you can't change at the moment. Tell yourself you will take care of the challenge in the morning. Don't let your mind keep you from getting a good night's sleep.

It's easy to get off balance with sleep habits by going to bed later and later each night while still having to get up early for work each morning. Lack of sleep leaves you feeling tired and causes you to reach for coffee or some stimulant in the morning. Going to bed late each night can make you sleep in a little longer each day, and you find yourself punching the snooze button, leaving less time in the morning for the little things that are important, like exercise or fixing a green drink. Feeling rushed at the start of a day puts you off on the wrong foot. Sticking to a schedule and establishing a rhythm can help you get a better night's sleep and have a happier morning.

If you don't sleep well at night, it's best to avoid daytime naps unless they are just short, twenty-minute power naps. Long naps rob you of good nighttime sleep.

Alcohol can put you to sleep in the evening, but it can also wake you up during the night or bring on bad dreams. So it's best to not drink too much or not drink close to your bedtime.

Here are some ideas for relaxing before bedtime: Take a hot bath and add some fresh rosemary, lavender, or even a few herbal tea bags. Listen to soothing music. Drink some chamomile tea. Don't work on your computer, and allow your mind to get into a resting mode.

By all means, avoid taking over-the-counter or prescription sleep medications because they have many side effects and can leave you feeling groggy. Before you resort to drugs, give yourself a chance to try natural ways first. There are many herb teas that can work to soothe you at bedtime.

I picked up a little trick while traveling: I sleep with wax earplugs every night. Not everyone can do this, but I find the little noises or (occasional snoring from my partner) is minimized with these little wonders. I also suggest high-thread count cotton sheets that are soft and light. Make your bed and your bedroom an inviting haven so you look forward to getting into it at night. An uncluttered bedroom and nightstand can help make a room peaceful.

11. WHAT REALLY MATTERS?

Maybe nothing will matter to us anymore when we leave this earth, but the quality of how we live and give of our self while we are alive will.

Our loved ones will inherit everything we ever bought or owned, but I believe what will really matter is what we leave behind other than the material. I believe what matters is what we give to others, not what we receive; what we teach, not just what we learn; how we empower others while empowering ourselves. The examples of *how* we lived will be left behind for our children and grandchildren and to our friends and loved ones. Making a difference while we are here by showing compassion for all living things and caring for our planet will matter. Letting the people we care about know we love them and being kind to those who need it will always matter, not only now, but long after we are gone.

12. MEDITATION CAN MAKE A DIFFERENCE

I started meditating in 1969, so I'd like to share what I know to be true. Meditation can silence the mind and bring inner peace. When your mind is clear, you are more productive. Mediation benefits the body, mind, spirit, and emotions. It reduces tension in the muscles and can reduce pain. It reduces stress, anxiety, depression, high blood pressure, and other ailments. It helps you live more in the present and not worry so much about the past or future. It gives you a deeper understanding of your inner self and your purpose in life. Meditation can slow the aging process and create better health, as it's known to stimulate neurochemicals that are associated with longevity. Meditation will increase self-awareness and induce happiness.

Meditation is easy to do, but it takes practice. Sometimes your mind is still and sometimes it is busy. Consistency and patience help make meditation easier. Here is a step-by-step guide on how to meditate:

1. You may sit on the floor with your legs crossed (called the lotus posture) or in a chair with a straight back. The important thing is that your back is straight and your body completely relaxed and comfortable. You will want to sit for 15–20 minutes.
2. Begin by relaxing the muscles of your face, then your neck, shoulders, arms, hands, and fingers. Relax your chest, abdomen, legs, feet, and toes.
3. Concentrate and focus on your breath and slowly inhale a full breath. As you breathe in, feel you are breathing in happiness. Let the feeling fill your body. As you breathe out, feel the breath is carrying away all troubles and worries. As you continue to breathe in and out, release your mind from every thought, concentrating only on your breathing.
4. The idea of meditation is to concentrate the mind on a single object. You may concentrate on your breathing, or concentrate on a mental or actual flame of a candle. You can use the mental image of a religious or spiritual

deity or use a mantra. Mantras are ancient energy-based sounds. They create a specific spiritual energy frequency and state of consciousness. Mantras can help still the mind.

5. You might notice after a few minutes that your thoughts have wandered. You may think, "Where shall I go tonight, or what shall I eat later?" When thoughts occur, acknowledge what you are thinking, let go, and bring your attention back to your breathing again.

6. Your technique is not as important as the idea of concentrating. This is what calms the mind and allows you to go to a deeper place inside yourself. Your mind will dance in many directions, but this is what teaches you that the mind is full of activity and needs meditation to acquire stillness.

I learned to meditate by using a personal mantra that was given to me by my guru. A mantra is useful to help you focus and keep the mind still. The word *Om*, which has many meanings, one being purification or peace, can be used as a mantra and is repeated over and over mentally or verbally to still the mind as the breath goes in and out. It may take some time, but eventually the mind will be quiet for longer periods. Sitting still and practicing meditation helps the meditation muscle, as I call it, get stronger.

Like physically working out, when you start, your muscles are weak, but over time your muscles become stronger. Because of meditation's rejuvenating process, it can make you look younger. Meditation helps you see the beauty in yourself and others and accept who you are on a profound and deep level.

13. INTIMACY

There are so many types of intimacy. There is intellectual and spiritual and there is sexual and physical intimacy. Intimacy is about closeness, warmth, affection, honesty, and familiarity. It's about understanding, fellowship, and affinity. It's about empathy and the ability to be loving and vulnerable. When you accept yourself, you can share intimacy openly with another person.

Knowing someone in-depth and allowing them to know you in the same way is sharing intimacy. Loving someone does not necessarily mean you are intimate with that person. It's possible to love someone and never let them in. It is possible to know someone for years and never spend the time or effort to find out what is meaningful to them.

We each have different ideas of what intimacy means. Our concept might be different than our partner's concept. Many people lose the intimacy they had in the beginning stages of their relationship. Relationships constantly change, and we sometimes forget to work at keeping intimacy alive. For women and men in a romantic relationship, a feeling of closeness, trust, and a place where you are accepted exactly the way you are helps create intimacy.

In friendships, you might have a natural intimacy with one friend because you trust this person and feel you can share your private thoughts. You can build intimacy by being open and sharing your feelings and letting someone know your vulnerabilities and concerns.

Intimacy is truly the basic ingredient of any meaningful relationship, whether romantic or platonic. To obtain intimacy, you have to keep sharing yourself and let others know you. Be truthful to yourself and don't be afraid to be vulnerable. If you live in fear and protect yourself or put on a front, if you don't let others know who you really are and how you feel, and if you don't trust others, then intimacy will slip by you and you will miss one of the most valuable experiences in life.

14. HOW TO BENEFIT FROM POSITIVE THINKING

Positive thinking is a mental attitude. It considers that there will be a positive outcome in any circumstance. It sees that health, joy, and happiness can prevail in any situation. When you have a positive outlook on life, you can cope better in challenging situations. Researchers have claimed that positive thinking can increase your lifespan, lower stress, and better your immune system.

Negative or positive, thoughts are continually running through our heads a million miles a minute. We imagine things are for the better or for the worse, and these thoughts affect our outlook on life. If we consciously work on thinking positive thoughts, we train the mind muscle to be optimistic. If we are worried all the time and think negative thoughts, we will train the mind muscle to be pessimistic.

Studies show our thinking can affect our health. When we think positively, our body language actually displays the way we are thinking. We stand straight, walk with sureness, and actually give off an aura of happiness and confidence.

Of course, at first it might not seem easy to think positively when something we consider bad is happening to us, or if we are experiencing one of life's challenges, but this is where we have to use the power of thought. When a negative thought arises, we have to replace it with a positive and constructive one. The negative thought might persist, but we just have to repeat the process and keep replacing it with a more positive one. Think of something pleasant that made you happy in the past. Get your mind off the negative. If you persist in this practice and keep ignoring the negative thought, your positive muscle will eventually strengthen and win out. Do not give up. Learn to expect the best, use your willpower to see the outcome you want, and keep practicing.

Positive thinking plays a large role in aging and health. Being hopeful about the future, enjoying life, and being happy all contribute to a longer life. Studies have shown that older people who think positive thoughts are less frail than those who think negative ones.

We all have a choice: We can decide to hold on to negativity and spend time talking to others about our woes and problems, or we can choose to talk about things that make us feel good and attract happiness. I've always said, "Your words can hear you." If you tell someone you get tired every day at 3:00 PM, guess what? You will be tired every day at that time.

Find a photograph of a happy time in your life and keep it close by so when a negative thought arises, you can look at the photo and remember what it felt like to be happy and positive. Remember, the choice is always yours.

15. LAUGH MORE

Laughing is one of the best medicines and actually makes us feel better. When we laugh, we send oxygen to our tissues and give our face muscles a workout. It boosts our heart rate, and it even burns a few calories. Laughing can lower blood pressure, reduce stress, and produces a general sense of well-being. Laughter is infectious.

In Norman Cousins's memoir, *Anatomy of an Illness,* he tells his story of being diagnosed with ankylosing spondylitis, a very painful spine condition. While bedridden, he rented old comedy films (maybe before your time) like those of the Marx Brothers' and episodes of *Candid Camera.* He credits laughter to helping him ease his pain. He said that after ten minutes of laughter, he could have two hours of pain-free sleep. Some hospitals around the country now incorporate laughter therapy programs into their regimes. Mark Twain said, "The human race has only one really effective weapon and that's laughter. The moment it arises, all our hardness yields, all our irritations and resentments slip away and a sunny spirit takes their place."

Need a laugh? Here are some ideas. Create a laugh night and rent some funny movies. Invite friends in for an evening, and let them know the theme of the evening is laughter. Have your guests bring something or plan on doing something that will add to the evening's fun.

Turn off the "bad" news and don't read the newspaper or watch news for a day or two each week. Practice smiling more and smile at yourself in the mirror when you pass by one. Learn just one joke that you can share with friends and family. Find humor in little things during the day. Go to a comedy performance occasionally. I find the more I smile at people, the better I feel. And they always smile back so I know I'm making others feel better also. A smile can bring laughter, and laughter can heal the soul.

16. TAKE A MENTAL HEALTH DAY

This should be a national holiday; everyone needs one once in a while. Yes everyone, even you. You work hard and go beyond the call of duty. You're always doing things for other people and for your job. You may get vacation days, holidays, sick days, but what you need for yourself is a mental health day.

No one is going to give you a mental health day off, so you just have to take one. This day should be about things you enjoy doing and enjoy doing alone. No cleaning the house or running errands, no phone calls to let everyone know where you are and what you are doing. This day is for quiet time, time for you, and a day for renewal.

You could go window-shopping or take in a movie. You could go golfing, go for a drive, exercise, or get a shave (or waxing) and a haircut. You could get a massage or go to a museum. You can sit in a coffee shop or get a pedicure. You can even stay cocooned in bed. Do whatever refreshes you mentally and gives you pleasure. Don't feel guilty, and don't think it's self-indulgent, but do indulge yourself. Don't say you don't have the time, just make the time. We all need to refresh our minds and body. You will feel so much better the next day and be more productive at work and with your family.

You need a mental health day every so often, so remember to take one before you get exhausted and stressed out.

17. BE GENUINE, HONEST, KIND, AND ETHICAL

If you're a spiritual person, being genuine, honest, kind, and ethical might be an easy thing to do. You might be honest and ethical because you believe in karma and the afterlife. You've learned that being a good person just feels better than the alternative, and you care about the world and everything in it. Even if you don't believe in the afterlife and karma, you might still be honest, kind, and ethical because you feel it's the right thing to do.

What interest would you have in being ethical? Maybe being this way might benefit your professional life. Is there some self-interest? We live in a world where everything we do affects something or someone else. We are all connected to the environment that we share. When we make a decision to not eat animals or recycle, we actually affect others with our choice.

If we have concerns about the planet we live on, then we, as individuals, must be ethical, sincere, honest, and kind. We must, regardless of the job we hold, be honest. We must care that the product we sell or the service we perform for our company is not harming people, animals, or our environment. We have a responsibility to ensure the product we sell is presented honestly and ethically. We can't base our presentation solely on self-interest or company interests, or can we? This is where personal ethics and honesty must prevail.

Some of the economic problems in the country today are caused by businesses lining their pockets without regard to employees or customers. Companies overcharge for products out of self-interest. They take advantage of their suppliers and customers and leave employees without livelihoods. For fear of losing profits, companies forget about loyal employees and forget about ethics.

Heads of companies and even philanthropic organizations have misused their power and ended up without moral values. The reputations of sports figures, politicians, businessmen and women come into question because their actions have been inappropriate. Do they publically apologize for their reputation alone, or do they apologize because they happened to get caught? Are they remorseful because they realized that they crossed the line of moral and ethical values?

Whatever the case may be, what makes some of us feel a responsibility to be honest and ethical? What makes someone start a foundation and be a philanthropist? What makes a business go beyond the legal requirements to enforce a code of conduct for their company? What makes a business leader become socially responsible? Is it karma, belief in the afterlife, or do they just know right from wrong?

For each of us, it is a choice we decide to make. For me, personally, it's a way of being. I think it all started when I was seven years old standing on my front lawn. A sense came over me, making my heart feel very open. This feeling made me realize the importance of being kind to everyone. What came over me that day has lasted my whole life.

It feels good inside to be kind to people and animals, to love oneself enough to tell the truth and to be honest. It feels right to have respect for oneself, for others, and the planet. Not for profit, not for fame, not for self-gain, but for the sake of integrity. It feels right to be genuine, kind, honest, and ethical. I believe these attitudes have side effects that bring about health, happiness, and a feeling of ever-lasting youth.

18. THE ULTIMATE RELATIONSHIP

Before you can have a good relationship with others, you have to have one with yourself. Some people don't have self-love because they think it's egotistical or selfish. Some people were neglected or abused as a child and find it difficult to express self-love. Low self-esteem creates unhappiness, resentment, obesity, and health problems.

Some people are quick to take care of everyone else including their families, bosses, and friends. They take the attention off themselves by doing nice things for others. Not until they are feeling overloaded and overwhelmed do they realize something is just not right.

In order to start practicing self-love, realize that you are the only one responsible for your experiences. Do not blame outside pressures, circumstances, or your childhood. You might have to learn how to nurture yourself, but you will start to see an immediate difference in the way you feel and gain power over self-doubt.

In my early thirties I was in a personal-growth workshop and we all had to ask the other participants what they liked about us. This exercise was a very important process for me as I was able to learn it was all right to appreciate my positive attributes and accomplishments. I was brought up not to say anything nice about myself as it would be considered bragging.

Do you pay attention when a friend pays you a compliment or says something nice about you? Start to listen closely to what others have to say and take it to heart. I guarantee, you will find out many good things you didn't know about yourself or had a hard time embracing.

When you learn to love and accept yourself just the way you are is when true self-love begins. Of course, you might want to improve your health or break bad habits, but while you're in the process, being self-critical does not support self-love.

Be a good friend to yourself. Be kind, thoughtful, and be a good listener. Be proud about your accomplishments and attributes. If you like making lists, make a list of all the things you like about yourself. This list is for your eyes only, so don't be shy. If you find it difficult to start this list, put down qualities you would like to see in yourself so you can start the thought process. Start to acknowledge things you do during the day that make a difference in the lives of others. Make a mental note of what you say to a friend or loved one that made them feel good. In turn, feel the happiness and love for yourself for contributing to another's joy.

See yourself through loving eyes and feel compassion for yourself. The love you want will not come from others but only from within yourself. It might take some strength to see the best in yourself and know that self-love is a good thing, but once you start the process, it gets easier and easier.

Look in the mirror and tell yourself, "I love you." Say complimentary things to yourself. Be nurturing and stop verbally putting yourself down. Listen to your words and stop negative remarks. Love what you see and see what is deeper than your outer appearance. Accept where you are in life and don't fret over aging; it's part of life's plan.

Let go of trying to accomplish too much in a day. Don't worry if you put something off. Don't try to be perfect in the eyes of others. Start being truthful to yourself. Find the things you do well and acknowledge yourself for all of your small and large accomplishments. These practices will teach you that you deserve to be loved, and best of all, you will begin to love yourself.

19. FINDING YOUR PASSION

What is life without passion? In order to discover what really makes you happy, you must discover where your passion lies. Passion is described as a strong feeling or emotion. It can drive you to succeed in your career or can drive you crazy in love.

When you find your passion, it can lead you to pure happiness. Your passion usually is tied closely to your interests. It can be associated with a talent you might have or something that might be easy for you to do. You might not realize that this "gift" of yours is something that others find difficult to accomplish.

When my children were growing up, I would tell them everyone is born with a gift. When you discover and use that gift, everything good in life starts to fall into place. Everyone has one or more gifts, and sometimes it takes years to find out what that gift is, but once it's discovered, you will feel passion everywhere you turn.

When you look at the things you like to do and things that give you satisfaction in life, and when you do these things and hours pass by without notice, then you're on to something. You are getting in touch with your gift.

Many who have not found their gift spend time at jobs that are not satisfying. Have you ever asked yourself, *If money were no object, what would I enjoy doing?* This question might be worth exploring.

I have a friend who needed a job. She thought she didn't have any gifts and had nothing special to offer, but when I pointed out that she gave the best parties around, she started to look at the situation differently. She realized her talent was putting people together and what she really knew how to do was have fun. She recognized how throwing beautiful parties made her and her guests happy. She was in her fifties and realized for the first time that this was one of her special gifts.

When we use our gift, we are supported by many surprising sources. We can expect the unexpected to happen. Money shows up out of nowhere, or resources appear out of the blue. People of like minds appear in your life. It's not a magic wand sprinkling fairy dust all over us, but it does feel like a dream come true. We can feel we are on the right path, and with a little work and effort on our part, doors will continue to open. Once we discover our gift and start to use it, our happiness level changes and our new attitude is obvious to everyone around us.

Joseph Campbell said in *The Power of Myth*, "All the time, it is miraculous, I even have a superstition that has grown on me as a result of invisible hands coming all the time—namely, that if you do follow your bliss you put yourself on a kind of track that has been there all the while, waiting for you, and the life that you ought to be living is the one you are living. When you can see that, you begin to meet people who are in your field of bliss, and they open doors for you. I say, follow your bliss and don't be afraid, and doors will open where you didn't know they were going to be."

Joseph Campbell also said, "It isn't merely a matter of doing whatever you like, and certainly not doing simply as you are told. It is a matter of identifying that pursuit which you are truly passionate about and attempting to give yourself absolutely to it. In so doing, you will find your fullest potential and serve your community to the greatest possible extent."

20. YOUR PEARLY WHITES, GUMS, AND TONGUE

White teeth, sweet breath, and healthy gums are important signs of a healthy body. After reading the list of ingredients on a tube of standard toothpaste, I had no idea what the ingredients were. The warning on the label said, "Do not swallow toothpaste." I always wondered what was in this commercial toothpaste, and how is it possible not to swallow any when brushing your teeth? Whatever is in the tube, I'm sure it gets into our body and mucous membranes when we brush.

I've been using natural toothpastes purchased at a health food store for many years. They are free of detergents, fluoride, synthetic colors, and preservatives. A couple of years ago, I started to research further and found a product I think really works best and it's called Tooth Soap. Everyone I know who uses it and have had sensitive gums say it relieved the problem along with many other gum and teeth challenges. At first use, I didn't like the soap taste, but by the fourth time, I didn't notice any taste at all.

Tooth Soap is little shards of pure soap; it removes any film on your teeth and makes them feel cleaner than any toothpaste I've ever used. I know it has helped my gums, because they used to be more sensitive when having them cleaned. After using the soap, the problem was gone, and my gums were no longer sensitive.

I have my teeth cleaned every four months just to be sure I keep my pearly whites.

I figure these teeth are the only set I can call my own, so it's important to take good care of them. I have all my teeth, including my four wisdom teeth, which I hear is quite unusual.

Diet plays a big part in healthy gums and teeth. I brush twice a day to make sure any sweet fruit I've eaten does not hang out in my mouth all day and throughout the night. We all know how important flossing is and don't ever think it's not. Flossing is vital for good overall health. By the time problems show up in your mouth, they have already had a head start in your body. Bacteria are easily eliminated with good dental habits.

Standard toothpaste has an abrasive ingredient that takes food stains off your teeth. Since Tooth Soap is not abrasive, every other day or so I use baking soda or a natural toothpaste containing neem oil. Neem oil comes from a fast-growing and long-living tree, native to Burma and India. It is known to be a natural way to whiten teeth and help cure gum problems. Neem oil is also used as a natural pesticide, insect repellent, and helps skin disorders. Neem is also used as a medicinal herb. Another helpful hint to help rid your mouth of bacteria is to rinse your mouth with hydrogen peroxide after brushing.

A friend from New Delhi, India, introduced me to an important asset of mouth and tooth health. It's called tongue scraping. He told me it was essential for the preservation of my teeth and overall health. Any white film on the tongue means bacteria are living there. Tongue scraping removes this problem and keeps breath fresh. Brushing your teeth does not remove white film on your tongue.

Yogis have been scraping their tongues for hundreds of years. A clean tongue activates the salivary glands and helps clean out bacteria when you have a cold or sore throat and helps you heal more quickly. Using your toothbrush to brush your tongue will only move the bacteria around and possibly make them stay on the brush, so for perfect dental hygiene, use a scraper, which can be purchased for only a few dollars on many Internet sites. A happy mouth and pearly white teeth will make you want to smile more often, so floss, brush twice daily, and see your dentist often.

21. MAGIC REMOVERS FOR PUFFINESS AND DARK CIRCLES UNDER YOUR EYES

Dark circles and puffiness can be a result of a poor diet, too much red wine, coffee, salt, or sleep deprivation. According to Chinese medicine, it can also mean a deficiency of the kidney.

I'll share a few quick beauty treatments, which can help minimize puffiness or dark circles around the eyes but are by no means a remedy for more serious problems. My mother taught me this one: put cold cucumber slices over your eyes to reduce puffiness. I remember as a child peeling a cucumber for our salad and using the peels to put on my face and eyes. It always felt so cool and refreshing. Cucumber slices cool the eye area and provide temporary relief from puffiness.

Rosemary tea made into a compress is another good external detoxifier. It boosts circulation and helps reduce any irritations around the eye area. Just make a strong tea with fresh rosemary and let it cool down. Use a cloth to soak up the liquid, and apply like a compress to the eye area. You can leave the compress on for 10–15 minutes and let the cool water be absorbed around the eyes by repeating the process a few times.

Putting slices of potato over your eyes will reduce dark circles. Place slices on your eyelids and lie down for 15 minutes. Wash the area when finished and apply coconut oil. The starch from the potato helps draw the toxins out. The coconut oil will take away any dryness the potato might have caused.

I was taught this next trick from an indigenous friend in Taos, New Mexico. To get rid of dark circles under her eyes, she makes a soft paste with tomato or pineapple juice, a squeeze of lemon, and some baking soda and pats this under her eyes. She leaves it for 20–30 minutes, then rinses it off with warm water, then very cold water. I recommend doing this several times to obtain desired results. You can also add a very small pinch of turmeric to the paste mixture for an added boost, just be careful not to get the mixture in your eyes.

These treatments will work if used regularly, but when dark circles or puffiness appear, don't neglect the signs. Clean up your diet and check your liver and adrenals. A detoxifying plan is usually a good idea to release toxins. When you get an outward sign of change in your appearance, just remember, something on the inside needs attention.

22. FLEX APPEAL MEANS SEX APPEAL

Richard Restak, MD, professor of neurology at George Washington University, says a daily one-mile walk reduces the likelihood of dementia by 50 percent. For many years I didn't exercise passionately even though I knew it was important. I would do yoga for months on end and then stop for one reason or another. I would take spinning classes for months, and then stop for some reason. I would do qigong and think it was for life, then stop again. Now I know for sure how vital exercise is to maintaining youth, vitality, and longevity.

Today, I consider myself a moderate exerciser. I include qigong, yoga, walking and hiking, Pilates, and some free weights. I prefer to do these exercise methods at home rather than a gym as I can pop a DVD into my computer or television and it's like having a private trainer. My favorite form of exercise is being outdoors, taking a long walk or hike with my boyfriend, family, or friends. On the way, I gather edible weeds, sage, and wildflowers.

23. KEEP THE SKIN ON YOUR BODY LUBRICATED

Over the years, I've tried many creams but always ended up going back to using my all-time favorite, 100 percent pure virgin coconut oil. Coconut oil is sold in a tub-like container, and when it's cold outside, the oil is a solid mass. When the weather is warm, it becomes liquid. I slather it on my face, neck, hands, and entire body. I use it after I get out of the bath and before I go to bed. I think it's the best treatment I've ever used for keeping my skin soft and lubricated. I also keep a tub in my kitchen and use it in some of my raw food recipes, including making chocolate. Coconut oil is healthy for inside and outside our body.

I don't use face base makeup and, shockingly, I don't use sunscreen anymore. I feel there are toxins and carcinogenic chemicals in many sunscreen lotions, and I also think it prevents the body from getting vitamin D, which is crucial to maintaining healthy bones and immune system, preventing certain types of cancer, controlling high blood pressure, and supporting the entire nervous system.

I like to get about ten to fifteen minutes of sun on my body daily in order to get my vitamin D, and I wear a hat if I'm going to be out in the sun during the hottest part of the day or when I'm hiking. We do need to protect our skin during certain parts of the day, so make sure to wear appropriate clothing. If you live in long-winter areas, vitamin D$_3$ is a good supplement to look into taking.

Our skin can dry out even when eating a healthy diet, so it's good to keep it soft and supple. I see many people walking around with cracked and dry elbows and heels when just a little care will alleviate this problem. When you massage coconut oil into your skin and nourish it, the results can be soft luxurious skin at any age. Your body will love you for it. I know mine does.

24. EXFOLIATE THE BODY

Thirty years ago, a Finnish doctor, Paavo Airola, suggested to his patients to dry brush their skin to achieve clean super soft skin. Today, this method is widely practiced in Europe. Dry brushing stimulates the lymphatic system, removes dead skin, and improves circulation. Dry brushing has been known to help in the removal of cellulite. I find it invigorating, and I know this is one of the things that made my circulation better.

If you can make time, do it on a daily basis as it helps shed your body of dead and dry skin. Using a soft natural-fiber brush with a long handle, dry brush in the morning before your shower or bath. Start from your feet and work upward, while always making long sweeping stokes toward your heart. Brush your feet, legs, body, hands, and arms. Stroking away from your heart puts extra pressure on it, so be sure to stroke upward and only toward your heart. Make sure to include your back and shoulders. It should take about 10 minutes to finish brushing your whole body. This is a great cleanser if you are feeling sluggish, and it's great for your lymphatic system if you are feeling ill. Brush lightly the first few times. The more often you dry brush, the more pressure you can start to apply.

25. EXFOLIATE THE FACE

A beautiful Russian woman I met in a health food store taught me a wonderful way to exfoliate my face. I use this method at least three times a week. It's gentle on the face and leaves it feeling clean and smooth. Pour pure vegetable glycerin, alcohol free, in a large bowl and add in salt a little at a time, mixing well until it's really thick and stiff. Store in a container and keep in your shower or on your tub. You can scent it with lavender or any scented oil you like, or use it unscented as I do. It's safe to use daily or whenever you need a good exfoliation. I use it on elbows, knees, and sometimes under my arms to open the pores and cleanse my armpits. I do not use underarm deodorant and don't have clogged pores, but it feels extra clean to exfoliate under the arms.

Another favorite face-exfoliation trick is a dry brush. Buy a softer brush than you use on your body. Find one that you can tolerate, and later you can always get a firmer brush for when your skin gets used to this kind of stimulation. Rub gently on dry skin in a circular motion. You will be surprised at how beautiful your skin looks after just one treatment.

A good way to use some of the almond pulp leftover after making almond milk is to rub the pulp directly on your face, and massage the mixture gently into your skin, adding a little water as needed. Rinse off the pulp with cool water. You can also grind up some almonds in your coffee grinder or spice grinder and wet slightly before rubbing on your face.

These methods of exfoliating will help rid your face of any dead or dry skin and will stimulate and bring life to pale, dull-looking skin.

26. KISSING SWEETLY

Bad breath, which no one likes to be on the receiving or giving end of, is a common problem produced by bacteria in the mouth. It could occur from food we consumed, including garlic and onions, or it could mean our system is toxic or sour. It's obvious that brushing our teeth twice a day and flossing and tongue scraping can help with some of these issues, but when you need a quick and natural cure for bad breath and don't want all those sugary and processed tablets sold at the checkout counter of your market, then here are a few hints.

Parsley is not just a decoration on your plate. It is full of chlorophyll and many other vital nutrients, including vitamin C and A. Parsley leaves contain beta-carotene for fighting free radicals, and folic acid, which is good for your heart. Just take a handful of parsley and chew it up as it's also good for sweetening your breath.

Of course it's not practical to carry parsley around with you, but to avoid over-the-counter tablets, you can mix cardamom seeds, fennel seeds, anise seeds and put them in a container to carry with you. Just chew the seeds and they will do the trick to rid you of offensive breath. You can also buy a premixed version at any East Indian store or online. In East Indian restaurants, the mixture is served in a small bowl with a spoon as you exit the restaurant. It's used not only for sweeter breath but also for digestion. Some mixtures contain bits of sugar, and some mixtures have only the seeds. The good news is they taste great, they work to sweeten your breath, and they are healthy.

Pineapple juice will also sweeten your breath as well as chewing on a few mint leaves.

If bad breath is a constant problem, it could be caused by a more serious toxic or sour system. I would recommend you try a good detoxifying plan. You can find detoxifying information on page 18.

27. GIVE YOUR FEET SOME LOVE

Unless you wear socks every day or get pedicures often, you will experience rough feet, especially in summer when you wear open shoes or go barefoot. Dry weather can make your heals cracked and callused. Here are some simple techniques that will give you great results.

For years I have used a pumice stone on my feet. I love the way they look and feel when they are smooth. I use my stone almost daily while bathing; however, you can use the stone on dry feet too. If your feet are dry and cracked, just rub the stone gently back and forth in a circular motion. Think of using a pumice stone like sandpaper, but don't get too rough and make sure you start slowly. If you would like to soften you feet first, do so in your bathtub or a pan of hot water, adding soap to help the softening process. While taking a bath, put soap on the pumice stone and rub the stone on your feet gently back and forth over the heels and the ball of your feet, including the tips of your toes. Don't forget the outside edges of each foot.

If your feet are exceptionally callused, it might take time to soften, but they will eventually feel smooth to the touch. Start by using the pumice stone three to four times per week. To help speed up the softening of calluses, rub your feet with coconut oil before going to bed. Be sure to put socks on to help keep the moisture in. The oil will help soften your feet while you sleep. Smooth feet will make you feel sexy and younger, and your tired feet will love all the attention.

When I get a pedicure, I never let them cut my cuticles. I request they only push them back. I've noticed when they are cut, it makes them harden faster as the cuticles are trying to heal from being cut. Just ask to have them pushed back, and in a short time you will see and feel the difference. Coconut oil works well on cuticles to soften them.

28. CELEBRATE YOUR BIRTHDAY FOR A WHOLE MONTH

Somewhere along the line, I think it was in my fifties, I realized that only one day was not enough to celebrate my birthday. Many people are disappointed on their actual birthday. They have this idea of what they want the day to be like and hope that others will fulfill their dreams, only to find out differently and before you know it, the day is over.

I love my birthday—always have. Since I started this monthlong affair, I've had the best time of my life. Everyone in my family enjoys celebrating the month along with me, or so they say they do. Try it out: give yourself the best month ever, do something nice for yourself every day. Celebrating the whole month of your birthday is quite fun. Let people know you will be accepting well wishes and presents anytime during the month. Even after the actual day is gone, you can enjoy the remainder of the month.

Celebrate others' birthdays too. It's so great to let people know you remember them on their birthday; tell them how much you care. Let them know you're glad they were born. Always celebrate a child's birthday. It makes them happy, and when they grow up, they will always remember how much fun their birthdays were. I always think that adults who don't like their birthday either didn't have good memories of that special day or don't like the idea of getting older. Bake someone a cake, bake yourself a cake (raw, of course), light a candle, and sing happy birthday. Celebrate life and enjoy every minute.

29. CLOSET CLUTTER

Research says we wear only 20 percent of our clothes 80 percent of the time. Something wonderful happens when you can walk into your closet and take a piece of clothing off the hanger and get dressed without trying on several outfits or looking for a piece of clothing you know is in there somewhere. When you have to try on several pieces of clothing and none of them really work because you don't have the top that works with the bottom or the belt that works with the shoes, you become frustrated. Any closet that's not organized makes your life confusing and cluttered. If you just had clothes in your closet that felt good and were flattering, it would make you feel better and be easier to maintain.

Clothes you don't love or are out of style or don't fit must go. Our bodies change, our lifestyles change, and styles change, so it's a constant upkeep. Even when you buy classics, they may no longer fit you properly, so have them tailored or get rid of them.

Professional organizers suggest you should start cleaning out your closet by inviting a good friend over to help you decide what to keep and what to get rid of. Mark a day on your calendar and get started. Take everything out of your closet. Make three piles.

Pile Number One is to donate or toss: these are clothes that don't fit you or your lifestyle, you don't really love them, or they just don't look good on you anymore.

Pile Number Two are clothes that fit your lifestyle, you love them, and they really look good on you. (This is why you need a trusted friend to help you.)

Pile Number Three are clothes you can't give away, you're not sure they look good on you, or they don't fit right now, but you think you will eventually fit into them again.

Put the clothes from Pile Number One, the donate pile, in boxes or bags, and load up your car so you can take them to your local thrift store or shelter. Take Pile Number Three and put them in plastic containers to store in your garage or spare room. Give yourself a set time that you will go back to the stored clothes, let's say six months. If you haven't thought about them or needed them by this time, you can probably get rid of them. Load them directly into your car and take them to a thrift store or shelter.

So now you have the "good stuff" from Pile Number Two left to organize. You can do this by color, season, or type. You can arrange all the tops and shirts, pants and slacks, dresses, or outer garments in groups and then by color. Try to use hangers that will not poke the shoulders out. Uniform hangers really make a closet look neater.

Even though your closet might look half full, you know you will be able to wear everything you have hanging there. Make a list of what you need to buy that might match a great pair of pants, or pants you might need to match a great shirt. When you go out to shop, you will know exactly what you need to complete an outfit. I promise you, this will make your life easier and calmer in every way.

CHAPTER 3

about
INGREDIENTS
and
EQUIPMENT

How to "Cook" Raw

If you've ever made a recipe from a cookbook before, raw food recipes are basically like following any other recipe. The only difference with raw food is some of the new terminologies, ingredients, or equipment used in preparation.

Most of you know how to chop up a bowl of fruit or make a simple salad. That's great for starters. The recipes in this book are meant to help you expand your love and knowledge for preparing raw food.

Don't be daunted if you see a long list of ingredients for a recipe; it does not mean the recipe is difficult to make or that it is time-consuming. Herbs, spices, and textures are important in raw food preparation, so a little of this and a little of that makes a difference for a delicious results.

1. Browse through the book for new ideas, and set a little time aside to try a new healthy way to prepare food. Let the photos in the book inspire you to try a new recipe. If you expand your horizons, these good habits will bring you a lifetime of health.

2. Keep your kitchen stocked with staples used repeatedly in many recipes. It will be easier to maintain a raw food diet if you have ingredients readily available. This is the same as stocking you kitchen with staples for cooked food.

3. Before starting to make a recipe, pull all the necessary ingredients from the cupboards and refrigerator and place them on the kitchen countertop. This makes it less likely for you to forget to include an ingredient and saves time in preparation.

4. Because you are learning a new way to prepare foods with new ingredients, choose the more complex recipes to make on a weekend or when you have more relaxed time, and try a recipe that seems simple to you.

5. Be adventurous, and make preparing food fun and not a chore. The rewards are great when you know you are feeding yourself and your family healthy energizing food. I always feel cooking with love permeates the food.

6. Feel free to embellish any recipe with your own creative ideas. When a recipe calls for "to taste," it means it's all up to your palate if you like more or less salt, pepper, garlic, sweetener, etc.

7. If desserts are your "thing," try a sweet recipe or two first. If you love bread, try a bread recipe. In other words, learn to satisfy your cravings with a healthy version of old favorite foods that are cooked.

8. Old habits are said to be hard to break. You learned to cook one way and now you are learning another. It will take a little time, but I promise you will get the hang of it, and it will seem easy and familiar after a short time.

Because of my love for travel and international foods, I've adapted many of my favorite cooked recipes from around the world into raw food pleasures. You will find them spread throughout the recipes section.

Food brings people together. Good food is good food no matter where in the world it originates.

When I was growing up, knowing about international food was an indication and privilege of those who traveled. However, with the blending of communities, cookbooks, television cooking shows, and availability of foreign-food products on market shelves, eating a variety of cultural food today is possible for many.

While at a trade show with my company some years ago, several friends and I decided for one week we would go to a different ethnic restaurant each night. Some of my friends had never ventured out before to taste foods from India, Ethiopia, Greece, Japan, or the Middle East. You can imagine how surprised they were when at an Ethiopian restaurant they had to break off a piece of *injera*, a rubbery-type bread, and pick up their food without the assistance of eating utensils. Needless to say, everyone expanded their horizons and opened their minds to food from around the world. It was life-changing for some, and for me, I always found it easy to find good vegetarian food in ethnic restaurants.

Although food from around the world is prepared in diverse ways with different spices and herbs, good cooks everywhere agree that food should be fresh and herbs and spices should be used generously. Guests are always welcome at the table and meals should be shared with family and friends. A raw food lifestyle incorporates all these attributes.

Ingredients

When mentioning ingredients, I am referring to organic and raw whenever possible. A couple ingredients used in my raw food preparation are not 100 percent raw. Some people feel fine about using these items and others decide not to, it's up to you.

SWEETENERS

There are several sweeteners on the market used in raw food preparation. The following are just a few:

Raw agave nectar is a natural sweetener taken from the agave cactus plant. It dissolves easily in other liquids and is claimed to be low on the glycemic index, making it safe for those monitoring sugar levels. Some raw foodists like agave, and others prefer different sweeteners. My recipes call for "sweetener of choice," but of course I do not mean white sugar or synthetic sweeteners. There are clear, light amber, and dark amber agave. I prefer clear as some claim it is the only really raw agave nectar.

Coconut sugar is not considered raw, but many raw food chefs use it because it is low on the glycemic index and is unprocessed, unfiltered, unbleached, and contains no preservatives.

Stevia is a nonsugar natural herbal sweetener and comes in liquid and powder form. It is used in baking and smoothies.

Date paste can be made by blending 1½ cups water and 1 cup dates. Blend until completely smooth. Date paste will last two to four weeks in the refrigerator. If a recipe calls for agave, you will need to double the amount if using date paste.

Yacon is derived from the root of a South American plant. It comes in syrup or powder form. Yacon is a good sugar substitute as it is glucose-free and does not increase blood sugar levels.

SEEDS

Flaxseed is rich in omega-3 fatty acids, high in most of the B vitamins, magnesium, and fiber, just to name a few of the benefits. In raw food preparation, flaxseed is a binder and when soaked becomes gelatinous. It is ground or used whole in many recipes. You can buy flaxseed in dark or light color, depending on what a recipe calls for or your personal preference. To make flax meal, grind seeds in a spice or coffee grinder or high-powered blender. Our body absorbs flax best in its ground state.

Hemp seeds are from the hemp plant and are full of nutritional value. They contain essential amino acids and fatty acids our body needs. Like flaxseed, when you purchase hemp seeds, they will have their hulls and shells

intact. Like almonds, hemp seeds make a great alternative to dairy milk. Along with vitamin E, hemp seeds are full of minerals, proteins, calcium, iron, zinc, and magnesium.

Sunflower and pumpkin seeds are high in iron, protein, calcium, phosphorous, and potassium. Sprinkled on a salad or used to make cheese, they add flavor and crunch to a variety of raw dishes.

Chia seeds are all commonly used in raw food preparation. Yes, chia seeds, like in chia pet. When soaked, chia seeds become gelatinous and are used to help foods bind together. Chia seeds contain many nutrients such as omega-3, fiber, and protein. Chia seeds make a delicious tapioca-type pudding. (See recipe on page 207.)

SODIUM CONDIMENTS

In my recipes I say to use "salt to taste" as everyone knows their taste buds best.

Himalayan or Celtic sea salt promotes vascular health, unlike typical table salt. We have been told that salt is not good for hypertension, heart problems, and other health issues. However, not all salts are created equal. Table salts are overprocessed sodium chloride and are kiln-dried, which removes naturally occurring minerals our bodies need. On the other hand, rock salt and sea salt are sun-dried and retain minerals beneficial to our bodies.

Tamari is a dark brown gluten-free liquid made from only soya beans that have undergone a centuries-old method of fermentation.

Miso is a fermented paste made of barley, rice, or soybean. Used for centuries in Japanese cooking, it is aged from six months to six years. Miso can be used in any recipe calling for nama shoyu or tamari by just adding water to thin.

Coconut aminos is a soy-free sauce containing seventeen amino acids. The taste resembles soy sauce, but it is made from raw coconut tree sap and sun-dried sea salt and is naturally aged.

Nama shoyu is a soy sauce produced by fermenting soybeans. It is not for those on a gluten-free diet but is used by many raw chefs.

Bragg's Liquid Aminos is a liquid protein made of soybeans and water only.

There are no additives, preservatives, chemicals, color agents, or added coloring. It is not fermented or heated and is easily digestible. It contains amino acids in naturally occurring amounts.

Nori is a toasted seaweed wrapper that is used in Japanese sushi restaurants. Look for raw nori sheets that are not toasted. Nori sheets are a staple in most raw food homes and used for making vegetable wraps. Like all seaweed, they are full of health-giving minerals.

Cacao butter is used in making desserts. It is a raw product produced without harsh chemicals and has not been refined in any way. It is never heated over 115 degrees and has antioxidant properties. Along with raw cacao powder and carob, cacao butter makes some of the best chocolate I've ever tasted.

Cacao powder is increasingly being consumed for its health-enhancing properties. It has been used in many cultures for thousands of years. Cacao powder is said to enhance physical and mental well-being and contains magnesium, calcium, zinc, iron, copper, potassium, and antioxidants. If you love chocolate, this is the guilt-free kind to use.

Cacao nibs are partially ground cacao beans. They are crunchy and have an intense flavor. They can be used to sprinkle on ice cream, eaten as a snack, or used in baking. Cacao nibs are full of antioxidants and trace minerals like magnesium and iron. In the raw world, many consider cacao nibs a superfood. Since they come directly from the cacao bean, they are partially fermented and low-temperature processed to take out some of the bitterness while keeping in all the nutrients.

Coconut oil: 100 percent organic virgin coconut oil is expeller pressed from the dried flesh of the coconut palm. It is free of solvents in the manufacturing process. Coconut oil is used in preparing many raw dishes, in smoothies, and is especially tasty in chocolate desserts. You can also use coconut oil on your face and body as a moisturizer and in your hair for conditioning.

Sun-dried tomatoes are fresh tomatoes that have been dried to preserve nutrients and vitamins. Because all the sugars get locked in during drying, tomato pieces have a rich-tasting, intense flavor. Dry your own tomatoes or find them already dried on the shelves at your market. Some are cut in half and dried and others are in thin strips. Sun-dried tomatoes need to be rehydrated in water before use. Sun-dried tomatoes packaged in oil are not the ones I am referring to.

Irish moss is seaweed that grows abundantly along the rocky parts of the Atlantic Coast of Europe and North America. It is most commonly purchased dehydrated and is usually light beige in color. It forms a mucilaginous body when soaked in water and is used as an emulsifying agent for thickening puddings, ice creams, deserts, nut cheeses, and soups.

To prepare dried Irish moss:

Cover 1½ ounce piece of dried moss with ⅔ cups filtered water. Soak twenty-four hours to soften. When it turns off-white in color and becomes swollen, it is ready. Drain, rinse, and pick out any dirt or sand. Cut moss into pieces and blend in water to make a smooth paste, adding more water if needed. Scrape down sides and inside of blender cover to make sure all pieces are well blended. Paste will last refrigerated for three weeks.

Sprouting is a good source of protein and an excellent way to get nutrients year round in your own kitchen. The germination process is simple, and all you need is a jar, a piece of cheesecloth, and some filtered water. Use sprouts on salads, in chili, and in making smoothies. Sprouts are loaded with vitamins, and the live enzymes are important to your health. (See sprouting instruction on page 115.)

Nuts used in raw food preparation are almonds, cashews, hazel, brazil, pecans, and walnuts. You might wonder why most recipes call for soaked nuts. The reason for soaking nuts and seeds is that soaking them releases the enzyme toxic inhibitors and increases the vitality contained within the nuts. When nuts are soaked, we receive more absorption of vital minerals and they become easier to digest.

Flour can be made from nuts and sprouted grains. Processing nuts in a high-powered blender, spice or coffee grinder produces fine textured flour. There are several methods to make flour, from soaking nuts and drying them, to using pulp left over from making nut milks. Nothing can hold back a raw chef from making delicious desserts and breads.

Nutritional yeast is not a raw ingredient, but is used in many vegan dishes to obtain a cheesy flavor. It is a reliable food source for vitamin B_{12} and protein. Nutritional yeast is deactivated yeast and is produced by culturing, harvesting, washing, and drying. It comes in flake form, is similar in texture to cornmeal, and works well in sauces, soups, on raw pizzas, breads, and in making nut cheese. Nutritional yeast is yellow in color and can be found in the bulk bins at your health food store. Do not confuse with brewer's yeast.

Lecithin is used as an emulsifying agent in many foods including breads, crackers, and desserts. With the recent introduction of sunflower lecithin, those avoiding soy products for allergies or soy's phytoestrogen characteristics can now use an emulsifier that is made using a cold press system that is raw and chemical-free. You will find the use of lecithin in some of my bread, pizza, and dessert recipes. Read labels to be sure you do not buy products with lecithin unless they say non-soy and non-GMO. I use Love Raw Foods sunflower lecithin that can be purchased online or at your health food store.

KITCHEN TOOLS AND EQUIPMENT

When adapting to a raw food lifestyle, you might not have all the equipment I mention. Don't let this stop you. You can substitute. If a recipe calls for dehydration, many times you can use an oven that is set on the lowest temperature and leave the door open. You can chop by hand if you don't own a food processor or mandolin. If you don't own a high-powered blender, use the blender you have and strain your drink through cheesecloth if necessary. Having the right tools and equipment makes preparing raw food easier, and when possible, I would recommend investing in good-quality equipment that last for many years.

High-powered blenders work best. Normal blenders seem to break down and overheat with frequent use. Making smoothies and sauces silky smooth are best done in a high-powered blender. A good blender is more costly than regular blenders, but in the long run, it will outlast five inexpensive ones. See product list on page 53 for names of high-powered blenders.

Dehydrator is a staple in a raw food kitchen. You won't need your microwave or oven once you start making raw food, but you will want to own a dehydrator. The stovetop is still used to warm certain drinks and warm water or to melt cacao butter, but other than that, a dehydrator should be considered if you plan to eat raw foods. You can purchase an inexpensive one, but like many appliances, you save money in the long run by buying the best equipment. See product list on page 53 for names of high-quality dehydrators.

Citrus juicers are a great kitchen tool to speed up juicing citrus. Lemons, oranges, and grapefruits provide many great vitamins. I have lemon and orange trees, so my juicer is an important part of my kitchen. During fruiting season, we juice and freeze so we can have citrus juice all year round. See product list on page 53 for names of my favorite citrus juicers.

Food processor: Most kitchens today have a food processor. Maybe you don't use yours very often, but when you start making more raw food dishes, it will become an important tool. Once you start using one, you realize how much time it saves and the special texture it gives many ingredients.

Spiral slicer is a kitchen tool that allows you to create spaghetti noodles and other fancy shapes from vegetables. Making raw food appealing will help keep you on track, and the spiral slicer just so happens to be one of my very favorite kitchen tools. A spiral slicer will turn an ordinary dish into a stunning presentation.

Julienne peeler: Ever wonder how chefs make those perfectly even slices and strips? A julienne peeler is a handheld kitchen tool that cuts vegetables into thin, even strips. Easy to use, all you do is drag the peeler across vegetables, and you will have sheets of even, small strips. Julienne peelers are fast and relatively safe.

Mandolin slicer is both a professional and home cook's kitchen tool. Razor-sharp blades make precise uniform slices, which make food appealing and easy to prepare. There are several different styles of mandolin slicers on the market. I prefer the adjustable platform-type slicer as I feel I have more control in cutting. Slicing becomes quick, and you will soon want to use it often for professional-looking vegetables.

Wire whisk is a stainless-steel tool with a handle and a balloon-type open wire top. It is used for whipping and incorporating air into a mixture, making texture lighter. It makes blending dressings and sauces a snap. I love having all sizes for different jobs, and I've always loved the way they look.

Ice cream makers are a nice addition to a raw food kitchen. You can whip up a batch of homemade ice cream in no time. Making raw ice cream is a treat, and most everyone loves ice cream. The best part is, you can make dairy-free ice cream without harmful chemicals or fillers. See product list on page 53 for product name.

WHERE TO SHOP FOR FOOD AND EQUIPMENT

Farmers' markets or local farmers are my first pick for fresh organic food, and health food stores come in second. I rarely shop in standard food markets unless they carry organic foods, but there is nothing like fresh, just-picked-that-morning vegetables.

Many raw food products are bought online, and delivery is quite fast. Sometimes prices are much better online than in markets. Here is a list of some of my favorite resources.

A variety of raw food products, equipment, and tools can be purchased at the following online stores:

www.oneluckyduck.com–Raw foods and equipment

www.therawfoodworld.com–Raw foods and equipment

www.ultimatesuperfoods.com–Raw foods and equipment

www.allissacohen.com/store/–Raw foods and equipment

www.gosuperlife.com/–Raw foods and equipment

www.rawfoodchef.com/–Raw foods and equipment

www.sirova.com/–Sea spaghetti, sea vegetables, raw foods

www.rawmamia.net/–Equipment

www.goldminenaturalfoods.com/–Sea vegetable salad, seaweeds

www.loveforce.net/–Raw bread and energy bars

www.amazon.com–Many items on Amazon

www.indianwildrice.com/–Hand-harvested wild rice

www.gnosischocolate.com/–Handcrafted chocolates

www.sproutpeople.com/index.html–Sprouting and microgreen seeds

EQUIPMENT I USE:

Dehydrator–9-tray Excalibur and 10-tray commercial Weston

Blender–VitaMix, model 5200 (I'm told Blendtec is also good.)

Vegetable juicer–Omega, model 8006 or VRT330 (I'm told Breville is also good.)

Spiral slicer–World Cuisine Tri-Blade

Food processor–Cuisinart 14 cup, model DFP-14CHN

Ice cream maker–Cuisinart, model ICE-21

Citrus juicer–Breville, model 800CPXL

STORING PRODUCE, NUTS, AND SEEDS

Most greens and vegetables purchased at farmers' markets or grocery stores are sprayed with water several times a day to keep them fresh. When we get them home and refrigerate them, they go bad very quickly.

The trick to keeping produce fresh is by shaking off the excess water and wrapping the greens and vegetables in paper towels. Place them back in dry plastic bags and store in refrigerator bins. You will find your produce last much longer and stay fresher.

Paper towels can be reused by hanging them to dry on hangers with clips. Reuse plastic bags or recycle them.

Most fruits and melons are best left on the counter until they are ripe, as refrigeration retards the ripening process. It's best to refrigerate fruits and melons several hours before ready to eat, or to keep them fresh after ripening.

Avocados are ready to eat when they have a very slight give to them. If they are hard when purchased and you need to use them quickly, place them in a brown paper bag and they will soften in two days.

Strawberries are very sensitive and rot quickly. The best way to store them is to pick over strawberries and remove any that have soft spots. Berries are best kept by storing in a closed container, single layer, with a piece of paper towel at the bottom to absorb moisture. Do not wash until ready to eat. Store in refrigerator and check daily to

remove any soft berries. Berries can also be frozen if you find you will not be using them in a couple days from purchase.

Fresh basil is best treated like a bouquet of flowers. Trim a little bit off the bottom of stems and place in a glass with water. Store in the refrigerator. Trim stems every two days to keep fresh.

Oily nuts such as macadamia, walnuts, cashews, almonds, and pine nuts are best kept refrigerated to keep them from getting rancid. Seeds such as flax and hemp should also be refrigerated.

Store other products such as dried berries, raisins, grains, spices, and powders in glass containers with a good-fitting lid. Wide-mouth canning jars work best. Jars can be placed in refrigerators or on cupboard shelves. Be sure to label jars when storing as it's easy to confuse grains or forget an unfamiliar item.

> **Never eat more than you can lift.**
> —Miss Piggy

Olive Oil Garlic Butter

CHAPTER 4

....

herbs,
SPICES,
and
CONDIMENTS

....

HERBS AND SPICES ARE AT THE VERY HEART OF GOOD FOOD

A plain dish can be turned into something quite exciting and robust with flavorful herbs and spices.

Herbs can cleanse your body of toxins and bring harmony to your spirit.

Herbs are used for medicinal, aromatic, and cosmetic purposes.

Herbs are made into rejuvenating herbal teas.

I prefer fresh herbs whenever possible and grow several different varieties in my garden. I also like to dry them at the end of the season so I always have some on-hand to spice up my recipes.

Organic dried herbs can be purchased at farmers' markets, health food stores, or online. You can easily grow your own in pots. The cost of drying or freezing your own fresh herbs is the least expensive and most satisfying way to enjoy them.

Making your own herbs mixture from fresh herbs is easily done. Fresh herbs can be dried to preserve their quality and flavor. Some herbs are best dried in the dehydrator if they are moisture-dense, including basil, mint, chives, and tarragon. Herbs that are low moisture include oregano, rosemary, thyme, marjoram, and dill and can be easily air-dried.

Harvest herbs in late summer before it gets cold. Pick in the early morning before they are wilted from the sun. If you are air-drying, tie bunches together at their stem end with a kitchen string or a twist tie. Place the herb bundle in a brown paper bag with the stem's end up. Tie the top of the bag and herb bundle close. Poke holes in the bag with a scissor or knife for ventilation. Tie the bag on a hanger and hang in a warm room with air circulation. Wait about two weeks before checking for dryness. When dry, keep a portion of the herbs separate and mix another portion together for use with specific dishes you prepare frequently. Store herbs in glass jars. Do not store near light or above a warm oven or dehydrator. Dried herbs are good for one year.

The following is a short list of herbs to familiarize you with some of the health benefits.

Basil—provides protection on a cellular level from radiation. Good for indigestion and bacterial growth. Basil has an anti-inflammatory effect. Basil has a concentration of beta-carotene and helps prevent free radicals from oxidizing cholesterol in the bloodstream. The smell of fresh basil always perks me up and reminds me of Italy. Basil is one of my favorite herbs.

Chives—are of the onion and garlic family. Contains vitamin C, calcium, iron, and potassium. Because of its mild stimulating effect, it improves poor circulation. I like chives in my salads, cheeses, and soups.

Cilantro—an energizing herb that can boost your immune system. Good for digestion and makes a nice addition to salads and smoothies.

Parsley—cooling for the liver, clears the eyes, and is a great diuretic. Curly or flat parsley make one of my favorite simple salads. I always feel energized after eating parsley, and because of its abundance of chlorophyll, it satisfies my craving for greens.

Rosemary—the oils in rosemary help to stimulate brain activity and alertness.

Good for your immune system and digestion. I have an abundance of rosemary growing in my garden and cut long stems to keep in a vase on my kitchen windowsill.

Oregano—is good for immune-building, bloating, and digestion. When used in tea, it has an antiviral decongesting effect. Oregano is one of the most used herbs in my kitchen.

Sage—enhances mental alertness and concentration by increasing oxygen to the brain. Sage can be used in a wide variety of dishes and always reminds me of hearty food eaten during fall and winter months.

Mint—there are many types of mint, and all are good for you. Mint helps digestion by just placing a large stem in warm water and letting it steep then sip as a beautiful fresh tea. Mint relaxes the intestines and settles the stomach. It's good for heartburn and helps support good vision. Mint helps eliminate toxins from the body and helps clean the liver.

I use mint in smoothies, deserts, and dressings. You will find a wonderful Aromatic Tea recipe on page 77.

I find it useful to mix some of my herbs together after they are dried to use in frequently made dishes. I also keep some of my dried herbs and spices separate for use with recipes I want to have a more subtle taste and then grind them just before use with a mortar and pestle.

We all have different taste buds. Some like salty or sour, peppery or sweet, savory or bitter. These suggested combinations should be tailored to your particular taste. Use more or less of any herb or spice that suits you. In making any recipe, always adjust herbs and spices to fit your taste buds. Five cloves of garlic may be too much for one person and just right for another. Always go with your instinct.

The following are some of my favorite blends:

italian mix

Italian herbs pair well with tomato-based sauces, breads, soups, salad dressings, stews, and pizzas. For a mixed blend, combine an equal amount of basil, thyme, marjoram, oregano, Italian flat parsley, and a smaller amount of rosemary and sage.

mexican mix

Mexican herbs pair well with tomato-based sauces, soups, dips, and salsas. For a mixed blend, combine equal amounts of cilantro, cumin, marjoram, oregano, and thyme, and a smaller amount of saffron, chili, and an even smaller amount of bay leaf.

asian mix

Foods most of us might be familiar with are Chinese, Japanese, Indian, and Thai.

Like all countries, Asian herbs and spices have their own special worldly taste. If you visit a marketplace in this part of the world, you will hardly recognize many of the foods or smells unless it is your place of origin. Most of us love Asian food, but we don't always make it at home. When you mix a small selection of five to seven of the following herbs together, you will achieve a delicious exotic Asian flavor: mix Chinese chives, cilantro, curry leaves, ginger, lemongrass, star anise, Thai basil, fenugreek seeds, cardamom, cloves, cinnamon, coriander, cumin, Kaffir lime leaves, turmeric, chilies, peppercorn, mustard seeds, coriander, mint, and tamarind.

indian mix

Specific for Indian cooking would be a garam masala consisting of a mixture of black and white peppercorns, cumin, cloves, cinnamon, cardamom, nutmeg, star anise, coriander seeds, mustard seeds, fennel seeds, ginger, sesame seeds, and turmeric.

moroccan mix

Exotic flavors, beautiful settings, and Moroccan food can be an experience to remember. Spices are rich and flavorful. This mix can be used in a raw-type couscous and other flavorful vegetables. For a mixed blend, combine two teaspoons each of ginger, cardamom, mace; one teaspoon each of cinnamon, saffron, allspice, coriander seeds, nutmeg, turmeric; and ½ teaspoon ground pepper, paprika, and chilies. Harissa is a paste made with garlic, chilies, olive oil, and salt. It is for those who like "fiery" dishes. Nuts, raisins, dates, and figs are used in many dishes, so you have a combination of spicy and sweet.

middle eastern mix

Unique flavors and colors are the foundation of Middle Eastern meals, and even just a little of these spices and herbs go a long way. For a mixed blend, combine a pinch of cumin, cardamom, nutmeg, turmeric, sumac (or lemon as a substitute), caraway, aniseed, paprika, allspice, and cinnamon. You can adjust these flavors and use more or less of any combination.

greek mix

Greek food is not spicy but very flavorful. Herbs are grown everywhere throughout Greece and the fragrance cannot be avoided. One can find herbs and spices growing on almost every kitchen windowsill. Salt is most popular to bring the flavors out of the food, and salt from the sea is of the highest quality. Pepper is on every table to add flavor to the food. No one herb or spice defines Greek food, but the most common ones used consist of marjoram, sage, thyme, oregano, basil, cloves, rosemary (used sparingly), thyme, mint, fennel, saffron, paprika, allspice, nutmeg, dill, parsley, coriander, bay leaves, parsley, cumin, cinnamon, anise, cardamom, coriander. You can combine a pinch or so of several herbs to make a blend.

herbes de provence

A beautiful fragrant French mixture I use quite often. Great in salad dressings, marinades, and soups. For a mixed blend, use a combination consisting of 1 tablespoon each marjoram, tarragon, thyme, chervil, rosemary, and summer savory. Use ½ teaspoon each mint, oregano, and finely chopped bay leaves.

sea mix

½ teaspoon Himalayan or Celtic sea salt

¼ teaspoon freshly milled pepper

1 teaspoon thyme

1 teaspoon basil

⅛ teaspoon garlic or garlic powder

½ fresh bay leaf, ground, or ⅛ teaspoon powdered bay leaf

1 tablespoon dulse, hijiki, or other seaweed

Mayonnaise,
Mustard,
and Ketchup.

Mayonnaise

MAKES 1 CUP

1 cup cashews, soaked for 3–4 hours

½ tablespoon apple cider

Pinch of salt

½ cup plus 1 tablespoon extra-virgin olive oil

2 tablespoons lemon juice

½ tablespoon agave or sweetener of choice

¼ teaspoon dry mustard, or homemade mustard (see recipe in condiment section)

Place all ingredients in a high-powered blender except olive oil. Blend until very smooth. Slowly pour in olive oil while blending until smooth and creamy. Add water if needed. Taste to adjust seasonings. Mixture thickens as it chills in refrigerator. Will last one week.

Mayonnaise can be used as a base for sandwiches, wraps, and dressings.

Mustard

MAKES ¼–⅓ CUP

⅓ cup yellow mustard seed, soaked in vinegar for 24 hours and then ground in spice or coffee grinder into a paste; or use 2 tablespoons dry mustard

¼ cup apple cider vinegar (use for soaking mustard seeds, then add 1 teaspoon at a time to taste)

1 teaspoon agave or sweetener of choice

1 tablespoon filtered water

¼ cup cashews, soaked for 4 hours, or Irish moss paste

1 shallot, finely chopped

½ teaspoon Himalayan or Celtic sea salt

Drain nuts and blend all ingredients in high-powered blender until smooth. Add water as needed. Taste for seasonings and adjust as necessary. Will keep in refrigerator for three weeks or longer.

Tip { Mustard gets spicier as it sets.

Ketchup

1 tablespoon cashews, soaked for 2 hours

1 medium-size tomato, coarsely chopped

3 tablespoons extra-virgin olive oil

½ teaspoon Himalayan or Celtic sea salt

1 cup water or more if needed to make a ketchup texture

1 cup sun-dried tomatoes, soaked in water for 30 minutes or until soft

1½ tablespoon apple cider vinegar

1 clove garlic, chopped

3 medjool dates, soaked in water until soft, or sweetener of choice

Place all ingredients except sun-dried tomatoes in high-powered blender and blend until smooth. Add sun-dried tomatoes and water as needed to make a thick, smooth texture. Store in a jar in the refrigerator. Lasts about one week.

Olive Oil Garlic Butter

Can be spread on raw bread or crackers.

4 tablespoons extra-virgin olive oil

1 clove garlic, crushed

2 pinches Himalayan or Celtic sea salt

Blend all ingredients together and freeze in a small ramekin. Let sit out just a few moments to make it spreadable like butter. Can be refrozen.

Dill Pickles

Almost like my momma used to make. As a little girl, I could never wait until the pickles were completely cured and would sneak one out the jar the day after they are made. My mother would call these "new pickles." It's the way I still like them, crunchy and crisp.

Pickles from this recipe are ready to eat in one day.

Enough pickling cucumbers to fit in a large mason jar

1 cup apple cider vinegar

4 sprigs fresh dill

1 teaspoon cumin

1 tablespoon whole peppercorns

1 chili pepper

English cucumber may also be used

1–2 teaspoons Himalayan or Celtic sea salt

1 sprig of thyme

3–4 cloves garlic

2 bay leaves

Filtered water

Wash pickles. Use whole pickling cucumbers or slice them in half lengthwise. If you are using English cucumber, slice into rounds.

Place 2 sprigs dill in bottom of clean large mason jar. Mix vinegar, salt, cumin, cloves, peppercorns, bay leaves, and chili pepper (optional) in a bowl. Taste liquid for saltiness and add more if needed, or wait until they are done and taste a piece of the pickle, adding more salt if necessary. I tend to undersalt, so you might want to use more. Pour spice liquid in the jar. Pack pickles around the inside of the jar, and then fill in the middle. Pack in as many as you can. Pour in filtered water to top of jar and place 2 sprigs dill and sprig of thyme on top. Put the lid on the jar and turn the jar over to incorporate spices. Store in refrigerator. I can't tell you how long they last, as we usually eat them all in a couple of days. They are ready when they taste good to you. Adjust spices if needed.

Double my recipe
for pickles if
you love them as
much as I do.

smoothies,
JUICES,
WARM DRINKS,
mocktails,
AND MORE

THE GREEN DRINK DAILY MOTTO

One of the questions I'm constantly asked is, "If you had to choose one thing to be healthier, what would it be?" My answer is always the same, a "green" drink.

Most of us do not consume enough nutrient-rich foods to build a healthy body. In fact, it's almost impossible to eat enough of the nutrients our bodies require on a daily basis. Many people end up taking supplements, hoping to replace what they don't get from their food, when supplements are not proven to always do the job.

All you have to do is commit to starting this process of changing how you eat. You don't have to begin by giving up anything; all you need to do is to start incorporating one thing from my plan. I call it

1. Drink a green juice or smoothie daily
2. Walk 30 minutes daily
3. Do 5 push-ups daily
4. Do 5 sit-ups daily
5. Stretch 5 minutes daily
6. Stay positive daily
7. Laugh daily
8. Love daily

"Changing the world one smoothie at a time."

One of the easiest and simplest ways to get all these nutrients your body needs is to consume a green drink on a daily basis. It is so easy and takes less time to make than the usual breakfast or stopping for morning coffee. This drink will supply you with energy lasting until late in the day.

Taking supplements is not as effective as having a green drink. Many supplements can be misused, resulting in toxicity and liver damage. You can get all your nutrients from a plant-based diet when including juicing and smoothies. Green drinks are not to be mistaken for juice you purchase in the market cooler section, which are processed and lack vital enzymes and nutrients. Of course, I would recommend a processed juice before recommending a carbonated sugary drink or coffee. Once you get used to making delicious green drinks at home, they will only take minutes and you will start to crave them. You will soon notice the difference in the way you look and feel.

Many people say they feel the positive effects after consuming their very first morning drink. Incorporating green drinks into your daily diet will help transition you into a healthier lifestyle. When you give your body the vitamins and nutrients it needs, desire for unhealthy and addictive foods drop away naturally.

Definition of a green juice: A green juice is made with a juicer. When fruits and vegetables are juiced, fiber is filtered out, leaving a very smooth liquid beverage. Pure juice is predigested and very healing for the body. All the nutrients and vitamins are captured even though the fiber is extracted, giving your body a rest from all the work it does to digest.

Juicing is better than well-chewed food because most of us don't actually chew our food well enough. Juicing helps build a strong immune system, raises energy levels and brain function. If we juice a raw carrot, we are getting all the benefits of the carrot, including beta-carotene (vitamin A), enzymes, and antioxidants. We get all the benefits into our system quickly to nourish our tissues, bones, and vital organs. The excess is passed quickly through the body, keeping our colon healthy and clean.

Definition of a green smoothie: A green smoothie is made in a high-powered blender. In a smoothie, filtered water is added to fruits and vegetables to make the drink of a smooth consistency. The fiber from the vegetables and fruits is broken down to minute particles. When you consume the drink, you slightly chew its thicker texture. Smoothies are a little quicker to make than juicing because the fruits and vegetables go into the blender jar roughly chopped and are blended in minutes. When you drink a smoothie, you have done something really good for yourself, and like pure juice, the smoothie helps sweep your colon clean.

Blended or juiced green drinks are full of needed live enzymes. Green drinks act as a blood detoxifier, are very low in calories, and are high in minerals. They are a source of chlorophyll and will give your skin a glow by flushing toxins and disease from your body.

Our bodies are maintained and kept healthy by how we digest the food we eat. We need enzymes to break down the food that enter our system. Our natural enzymes can be depleted over time and our bodies do not produce new ones, so we need to add them to our daily diet. When we drink a green drink, we are absorbing pure enzymes from the fruits and vegetables.

I'm often asked if eating a fruit or vegetable is just as healthy for you as making a green drink. Of course eating fruits and vegetables (a nice apple or carrot) would provide nutrients, but we could never eat enough in a day to get all we need or chew the fruits and vegetables well enough to extract all the nutrients before it passed through our body. I've found nothing is as beneficial as a daily green drink. It can pack more nutrients in one drink than we can consume in a plate of salad. One large glass of juice can supply us with more nutrients than we could get from eating three vegetable meals a day. By having one green drink every day, we can consume many more fruits and vegetables than we could ever eat.

A drink could contain apple, celery, cucumber, broccoli, red bell pepper, and spinach. This one drink alone provides us with a wide variety of daily vitamins, minerals, phytochemicals, and micronutrients, and it's all predigested. Yes, it's good to eat salads and whole fruit, but not in place of green drinks. I find a green drink in the morning and a big vegetable salad for lunch or dinner is a perfect combination.

There are endless combinations of green juices and smoothies. Once you get started, you will quickly be creating your own.

Tip { Add greens to any smoothie drink, along with goji berries, maca, hemp seeds, and fresh berries for more antioxidant and nutritional value.

When selecting organic fruits and vegetables for green drinks, purchase fresh, brightly colored produce without bruises. Buy local fruits in season when they are at their peak and less expensive. Freeze fruits in season to enjoy in smoothies long after they are gone from the market.

One of my favorite fruits to freeze is bananas. When they are ripe and spotted with brown specks, peel and freeze in an airtight container or ziplock bag. Bananas are perfect to sweeten up any smoothie. Markets put spotted bananas on a discount rack in the produce department, and these are perfect for freezing as their natural sugars are at their peak. If you find a large blackened area where the banana is soft to the touch, it is usually a bruise and you can cut the spot out before freezing.

Freeze berries or fruit in containers that will be moisture-resistant and easy to seal. I use plastic freezer ziplock bags or snap-lid glass containers. To prepare fruit for freezing, pick over and discard any bruised or soft spots. Lightly wash and pat dry. Remove pits and stems. Berries can be frozen whole while other fruits might need to be cut into pieces. Freeze small portions that can be used completely from the container to make one or two smoothies. The secret of keeping fruits and berries separated and not frozen into one lump is to place them on a baking sheet, not touching each other, and freeze for twenty to thirty minutes to harden, then place them in individual containers to store in the freezer.

Basic Green Smoothie

SERVES 1

1 apple or pear, cut in large pieces   2 stalks celery, cut in large pieces

2 handfuls of spinach or other dark leafy greens

Add 1 or more cups of water to blend very smoothly.

Optional:

½ banana, frozen   1 handful blueberries, strawberries, or goji berries

Place all ingredients in a high-powered blender.

Power Greens

SERVES 2

I like this juiced instead of blended. However, if you blend, be sure to add 1½ cups of water.

2 apples   3 romaine lettuce leaves

3 stalks celery   2 kale leaves, stems removed

2 handfuls of spinach   1" piece of ginger, peeled

½ fennel bulb   ½ lemon, peeled

1 cucumber

Juice, or if blended in a high-powered blender, add water for desired consistency

Tip { Let your imagination run wild!

Tangerine Green Smoothie

SERVES 1

2 tangerines

1 green apple

1 banana, frozen if possible

2 kale leaves, stems removed

Small handful spinach

1 to 1½ cups water or enough to blend into a smooth texture

2–3 medjool dates, to sweeten

Small handful cilantro

Add ice if you like and blend until smooth.

Simple Green Drink

SERVES 2

2 Thai baby coconuts, use water only (the meat can be frozen for other uses)

2–3 frozen bananas

2 large handfuls spinach

Blend in high-powered blender.

Tip { Fresh Thai baby coconut water is good for hydration and contains electrolytes. I love using coconut water in my smoothies in place of water. Purchase from your local Asian market, health food store, or online. Boxed coconut milk can be purchased at health food store, but in my opinion, fresh tastes best.

Trip to the Moon

SERVES 1–2

1 Thai baby coconut, water only

2 peaches, plums, or nectarines

Handful of seasonal berries

6 kale leaves, stems removed

Add ice and blend until smooth. If you like a sweeter taste, add 2 medjool dates, pitted. Add water if needed.

Granny's Smoothie

SERVES 2

2 Granny Smith apples, roughly chopped

½ cucumber, peeled and roughly chopped

2 handfuls spinach

1½ cup pure water

Blend in a high-powered blender until smooth. Add ice and blend again if desired.

Mango Smoothie

SERVES 2

2 cups mango, chopped

1 lime, juiced

1 green apple, chopped

1 tablespoon chia seeds, covered with water and soaked to make a gel

1 cup Thai baby coconut water or filtered water, with

1 tablespoon virgin coconut oil

1–2 handfuls of dark leafy greens of choice

3 medjool dates, pitted

Add all ingredients to high-powered blender.

Watermelon-Honeydew Smoothie

SERVES 2–4

3 cups watermelon

1 honeydew

Place in blender and push down sides until the melon extracts enough juice to blend on its own. When blended, add 1 cup ice and blend until thick. Sweetener can be added if desired.

Serve in tall glasses with a straw.

Tropical Smoothie

SERVES 2

½ pineapple, cut into pieces

1 cucumber, cut into pieces

1 lime, peeled

1 large handful of spinach

1 tablespoon virgin coconut oil

1 grapefruit, peeled

2 teaspoon avage, or sweetener of choice

Blend in high-powered blender and add pure water as needed. Add 1 cup of ice and blend well.

What a Pear

SERVES 2

2 ripe pears

1 cup celery

1 cucumber

1 lemon, peeled

1 lime, peeled

1" piece ginger

Blend until smooth and add water as needed. Add ice and blend again

Banana Mania

SERVES 2

3 bananas

2 granny smith apples, coarsely chopped

4 kale leaves, stems removed

1 lime juiced

1 handful spinach leaves

Blend, adding pure water as needed. Add ice and blend again.

Berries and Chocolate

SERVES 2

1½ cup mixed berries in season

1 orange, peeled

1 stalk celery

½ cucumber

½ banana, frozen

1 tablespoon cacao powder

1 cup pure water

1 tablespoon agave, 2 dates or sweetener of choice

Blend well. Add ice and blend again.

Summer Celebration

SERVES 2

1 large mango

1 pomegranate, juiced

2 cups filtered water

½ pineapple

1 tablespoon sweetener of choice

Ice as desired

Place all in blender and blend until smooth.

Nut milks

The healthiest and most delicious nut milks are homemade and quite simple to make. Nut milk has many uses, including sauces, gravies, smoothies, ice cream, pies, cakes, in cereals, and even a glass with a great raw cookie or two.

Almond milk contains vitamin E, potassium, copper, and magnesium. It's lower in calories than dairy milk, and one glass is approximately 70 calories. Almond milk is healthier for you than soy or rice milk, and I think the taste is much better. Nut milks are healthier for you than cow's milk and do not contain any residual steroids or hormones.

Nut milks are easy to make at home. They are lactose and gluten free, and they do not contain saturated fats.

Other favorite milks are brazil nuts, cashews, and hemp seed.

Almond Milk

MAKES 3 CUPS

1 cup almonds, soaked overnight	2 medjool dates, pitted
3 cups filtered water (more if you like it thinner)	½ teaspoon vanilla, or seeds from vanilla bean

Strain soaked almonds and place in a high-powered blender. Add water, dates, and vanilla and process until smooth.

Pour the milk into a nut filter bag, which can be purchased online, or use cheesecloth to strain. If you don't have either on hand, use a fine-screen strainer. Squeeze all the liquid from the pulp into a bowl. A filter bag is inexpensive and good to own as it's the easiest way to extract all the milk, leaving the pulp in the bag. Pulp can be stored in freezer for later use in making flour for cakes, breads, and cookies.

Store milk in glass jar with lid and refrigerate. Good for 3–4 days.

Cacao Almond Milk

MAKES 3 CUPS

1 cup almonds, soaked overnight

3 cups filtered water

2 medjool dates, pitted

½ teaspoon vanilla, or seeds from vanilla bean

Strain soaked almonds and place in a high-powered blender. Add water, dates and vanilla and process until smooth.

Pour the milk into a nut filter bag, which can be purchased online, or use cheesecloth to strain milk. If you don't have either on hand, use a fine-screen strainer. Squeeze all the liquid from the pulp into a bowl.

Add the following:

⅓ cup cacao powder	2–3 tablespoons agave or sweetener of choice, or to taste

Blend well.

Banana Cacao Smoothie

SERVES 1

1 cup almond milk	1 tablespoon raw cacao powder
1 banana, preferably frozen	1 tablespoon agave, maple syrup, coconut sugar, or 2–3 dates
1 teaspoon maca (optional but very good for hormonal balance)	

Add a generous scoop of ice to make it thick and frothy and blend until smooth.

Alternative method if you don't have almond milk:

1 banana	1 tablespoon agave or 2–3 dates
1 teaspoon maca	1 cup water or more if needed
1 tablespoon raw cacao powder	
¼ cup almonds or 1 tablespoon raw almond butter	

Add a generous scoop of ice to make it thick and frothy and blend well.

Orange Ice Smoothie

SERVES 1

2 oranges, peeled and seeded	1 teaspoon vanilla extract or scraping from inside ½ vanilla bean
1 cup almond milk	
3–4 dates, pitted	

Add a generous scoop of ice and blend until thick and slushy.

Alternative:

Use 2 tablespoons raw almond butter and 1 cup of water to replace almond milk.

Carrot Nog Smoothie

This is one of my favorite holiday drinks.

SERVES 1

1 cup almond milk	Sweeten with agave or 2 pitted medjool dates.
½ cup carrot juice	

Add a large scoop of ice to thicken the drink and blend in a high-powered blender. Sprinkle in nutmeg and cinnamon.

Aromatica Tea

SERVES 1

I learned to make this drink while traveling in Bogota, Colombia.

- 3–4 stems of fresh mint
- 1 small slice crisp apple
- 1 strawberry, cut in half
- 1 small piece of guava or mandarin orange
- 5–6 chamomile flowers
- 3–4 hawthorn berries

If you cannot locate chamomile flowers or hawthorn berries, replace with a chamomile tea bag.

Warm water for tea. Let it cool down to where it's drinkable before adding tea bag.

TO SERVE

I like to use a bowl smaller than a soup bowl and larger than a rice bowl.

It should feel comfortable to hold between both hands. The reason for the bowl is for the release of the aromatic fragrance and so you can see all the beautiful fruit and herbs.

Place the mint leaves in the bowl and add the balance of the fruit and herbs. Slowly pour the warmed water into the bowl.

When serving for more than one, put a stalk of mint and tea bag in the water while it's cooling down.

Feel free to alter any of the fruit or herbs. I make a more savory Aromatica Tea with lavender, sage, and thyme.

Aromatica Tea is a perfect afternoon pick-me-up, a soothing late-evening drink, and a wonderful after-dinner soother.

Maca Coffee

SERVES 1

- 1 cup pure water, warmed
- 1 tablespoon maca powder

Whisk while adding the following:
- 1 tablespoon agave or sweetener of choice

Whisk in ¼ cup almond milk or more if desired.

In a double boiler or pot on the stove, heat water until warm (do not overheat). Add all ingredients and more sweeteners to taste if necessary and whisk together to incorporate.

Hot Chocolate, Only Better

SERVES 2

This is a great cold-day treat.

- 3 cups homemade almond milk
- ⅓ cup raw cacao powder
- 2–3 tablespoons agave, or sweetener of choice, to taste
- 1 tablespoon grated cacao butter

Slightly warm milk in a double boiler or pot on the stove so it is just warm to the touch. (Do not overheat.) Add cacao powder while whisking. Continue whisking to incorporate cacao. Add sweetener and grated cacao butter.

Spiced Chai, Warmed (or Iced for Summer)

SERVES 2

2–3 cups warm water

1 decaffeinated green tea bag or other tea or herbs of choice

½ teaspoon fresh ginger, grated, or ⅛ teaspoon ginger powder

1 cinnamon stick, or ⅛ teaspoon ground cinnamon

3 whole cloves, or a pinch of ground cloves

1 cardamom pod crushed or grated, or 1 pinch ground cardamom

1 star anise

3 grinds of fresh black pepper

In a double boiler or a glass jar in dehydrator, warm water. If you heat in a pot on the stove, make sure it is just warm to the touch. (Do not overheat.) Add all ingredients, put a lid on the pot, and let tea steep for about 1 hour. Add agave or sweetener of choice to taste. Add ⅓–½ cup almond milk, and slightly warm to drinking temperature. Adjust seasonings, making it sweeter or spicier to your taste. Strain before drinking.

This drink is best chilled overnight to meld all the spices.

Tip To give the tea a thick texture, make almond milk using 1 cup soaked almonds, drained, and add to blender with 1½ cups water, 2 medjool dates, and blend until smooth. Strain through nut filter bag and use in Chai Tea. Store the remaining milk in a closed jar in the refrigerator. Make a double batch of chai tea as it's great the next day, especially iced.

Warm Apple Chai

SERVES 3

3 cups fresh apple juice

⅛ teaspoon cinnamon or 1 cinnamon stick

Pinch of ground cloves or 3 whole cloves

1 star anise

⅛ teaspoon powdered ginger

In a double boiler or a glass jar in dehydrator, warm apple juice. If you heat in a pot on the stove, make sure it is just warm to the touch. (Do not overheat.) Add all ingredients, put a lid on the pot, and let it steep for about 1 hour. Warm again and enjoy.

raw food chefs from around the world share one of their special drinks

I invited some of my favorite and most respected raw food chef friends to contribute a recipe for a healthy drink to promote youthfulness. Some ingredients may be unfamiliar, but if you want to kick-start your health, be sure to look up these ingredients online and learn a little from the experts.

Sarma's "Green Mango" Shake

SERVES 3–4

2 cups fresh mango, diced

2 cups coconut water

1 cup cucumber, chopped and peeled

3 tablespoons of lime juice

3 tablespoons agave nectar or 2 packets stevia

2 teaspoons vanilla extract

1 small handful fresh cilantro leaves

Pinch of sea salt

In a blender, puree all ingredients until smooth.

Sarma Meingaillis is cofounder, proprietor, and president of New York City's first upscale raw food restaurant, Pure Food and Wine. She is owner of One Lucky Duck, which is a takeaway retail store around the corner from Pure Food and Wine and recently opened an outpost at Chelsea Market. Sarma is the author of two books: her most recent, *Living Raw Food*, and her earlier book, coauthored with Matthew Kenney, *Raw Food Real World*. Her gourmet food at Pure Food and Wine and One Lucky Duck are outstanding, and the restaurant patio is simply the most beautiful and romantic setting. Website: http://www.oneluckyduck.com and www.purefoodandwine.com

Chef Ito's Super Lunch Drink

SERVES 2

2 cups fresh Thai baby coconut water

1 tablespoon pure barley green powder

1 tablespoon Quantum Green Mix Powder (Premier Research Brand)

1 tablespoon fresh coconut cream/powder

1 tablespoon Spirulina powder

1 tablespoon Blue Manna powder

½ cup raw noni juice

Blend together in a high-powered blender.

The amazing and always cheerful **Chef Ito** creates his incredible vegetarian, vegan, and living food dishes at Au Lac Restaurant in Fountain Valley, California. Au Lac has an Elixir Cocktail menu (sans liquor), and Ito's food and desert creations are sheer art in presentation and taste. Chef Ito took a vow of silence seven years ago and his words come through his food with so much love. If you're lucky, you might even get one of his quick massages or a bit of the special oils he creates. Just to be in his presence makes me happy and I just love his food. Website: **www.aulac.com**

Alissa Cohen's Neroli Blossom

SERVES 1-2

Neroli hydrosol is made from bitter orange blossoms. Look for it in health food stores. The combination of pineapple, coconut, and mint with banana is already great, but the neroli gives this a unique taste of orange blossoms.

¼ cup ice	1 teaspoon fresh mint, chopped
¼ cup coconut water	1 banana
1 cup pineapple chunks	1 teaspoon neroli hydrosol

Blend together in a high-powered blender until smooth.

Alissa Cohen is an internationally recognized author, speaker, raw food chef, restaurateur, nutritional consultant and mind-body therapist. Her books, *Living on Live Foods* and *Raw Food for Everyone,* are a testament to her skills as a raw food chef. Allisa's online store sells a variety of products for health, beauty, and home. Website: www. allissacohen.com

Russell James's Aloe Lemonade

SERVES 4

32 oz. springwater	1-2 pinches salt
1-2 lemons, peeled	1-3 tablespoon agave or sweetener of choice
½-1 aloe leaf	

Peel the lemons to get off as much yellow skin as you can while leaving on as much of the white pith as possible. Also filet your aloe vera so that only the inner gel is remaining. Add springwater and lemons to the blender. Blend for 40–60 seconds and then strain off the pulp. Next add a few dashes of salt, your aloe filets, and your sweetener of choice. Blend and enjoy!

Russell James was born in England. He is an international raw food chef and instructs men and women worldwide through his blog, eZine, live food classes, and home study DVD course. He recently was a guest instructor at 105degrees, a raw food restaurant and school operated by Matthew Kenney in Oklahoma. www.therawchef.com

Raw Chef Dan's Green Dream

1 medium cucumber	1 medium pear
2 stalks celery	1" piece of ginger
3 leaves kale, stem removed	Juice of ½ lemon
3 leaves arugula or spinach	

Juice. If you blend in high-speed blender, add pure water to make a smooth mixture.

Raw Chef Dan opened the Quintessence raw food restaurant in New York City in 1999. His newsletter, blog, and videos are helpful for anyone wanting to learn more about raw food, and his restaurant is not to be missed on a trip to New York. Website: www.rawchefdan.com/raw chef dan/resume.html

Matthew Kenney's Pineapple-Aloe Smoothie

SERVES 2

1 cup fresh pineapple, chopped

½ cup ripe banana, frozen and chopped

1 teaspoon virgin coconut butter

Pinch cayenne pepper

1 tablespoon fresh aloe (gel)

Pinch of lime zest

½ vanilla bean, seeded

8 oz. coconut water

1 tablespoon raw agave or sweetener of choice

Small pinch sea salt

Blend well, at least 1 full minute, and garnish with pineapple wedge.

Matthew Kenney is a chef, author, entrepreneur, restaurateur, and director of Culinary Arts and Operations for 105degrees in Oklahoma. His company, Matthew Kenney Cuisine, is focused on the development of products, books, and businesses that reflect a growing interest in sustainable cuisine. His role is creative, with an emphasis on a modern approach to menu development, design, branding, and marketing. Website: www.105degrees.com and www.matthewkenneycuisine.com

Smoothie Girl and Shitake Present Vanilla Sky Smoothie

1 cup organic raw unsalted macadamia nuts (preferably soaked overnight)

1 teaspoon organic vanilla essence or the scraped pod of half a vanilla bean

5 ounces of organic frozen pineapple pieces

1 dessert spoon of organic raw agave or 2 organic medjool dates

Place all ingredients in a blender and blend until smooth.

Optional (for those not vegan)

1 teaspoon of Manuka Honey ("Active" honey with a 20+ rating or higher is more potent/medicinal.)

1 teaspoon of bee pollen

Omid Jaffari styled and photographed vanilla sky smoothie photo. He is an international botanical chef and the creator of Shitake and Tried. Tasted. Served. Website: www.triedtastedserved.com, www.shiitakeblog.com

Lucy Stegley is the co-coordinator of Australia's first raw, vegan-friendly university campus cafe, *Realfoods*. Her alter ego, *SmoothieGirl,* blends up scrumptious smoothies based on organic seasonal produce. Website: www.raweventsaustralia.com and www.su.rmit.edu.au/departments/rusu-realfoods.

Tip { Adding the optional celery or lettuce to your smoothie will add minerals and help balance the sweetness of the fruit.

Mia's Knock the Years Off Smoothie

SERVES 1–2

12 kale leaves

1 cups fresh pineapple

1 banana

1 pear

1 apple

1 lemon

1 oz. wheat grass

4 leafy stems of mint

1 ½ cups of purified water

8 ice cubes

In a high-powered blender, add water, banana, kale, and pineapple. Blend until broken down. Add pear, apple, lemon, mint, and ice. Blend until smooth. Yummy!

Mia Kirk White is a Certified Holistic Health Counselor. She holds degrees in Jin Shin, Swedish massage, and acupressure. She teaches classes on healing through whole plant-based foods. Helping to create better eating habits for children, Mia works with families in person, online, and by phone. Website: www.rawmamia.net E-mail: rawmamia@comcast.net

Cherie's Peaches 'n' Cream

YIELD: 4 CUPS (2 SERVINGS)

Some flavor combinations are always winners and peaches and cream is one of those. This delightful smoothie is rich and satisfying and will hold you contentedly until lunchtime. It also makes a fabulous afternoon snack!

1 cup nonchlorinated water

4 cups fresh ripe peaches (or nectarines), pitted and chopped

2 oranges, peeled and chopped

½ cup raw cashews, soaked in 1 cup water for 1–2 hours and drained

Water to thin, as needed

Blend the peaches, oranges, and cashews in a high-powered blender, adding water to thin. Serve immediately.

Cheri Soria is the founder and director of the prestigious Living Light Culinary Institute and author of three books including, *Raw Food Revolution Diet*. Cheri has been teaching raw vegan culinary arts to students and teachers from around the world since 1992 and has been the inspiration to a generation of raw food chefs and authors. She is known as the "mother of gourmet raw cuisine." www.rawfoodchef.com–for information about certification courses.

Tip { Adding the optional celery or lettuce to your smoothie will add minerals and help balance the sweetness of the fruit.

Ani's Ginger Lime Aid

MAKES 8 CUPS (ADAPTED FROM ANI'S RAW FOOD ESSENTIALS)

1 tablespoons ginger, minced

⅓ cup lime juice, from
   approximately 6 limes

½ cup honey, agave, or maple syrup

8 cups sparkling water

1 cup ice

Place ingredients into your high-speed blender, except the ice, and blend smooth. Add ice, and blend to mix. Serve immediately.

Ani Phyo is one of the prominent experts in the raw food community and author of *Ani's Raw Food Essentials*, *Ani's Raw Food Kitchen* and *Ani's Raw Food Desserts*. She has won numerous awards and hosts an uncooking show on YouTube. Website: www.AniPhyo.com

IT'S MOCKTAIL TIME

You come home from a hard day's work, put your feet up, and you are ready to have a cocktail. But alas, you remember you have turned over a new leaf and decided to put your health first. What to do? Well do not fret for I have invented the "Mocktail," a healthy alternative, and served in your favorite glass with a creative imagination, you might even feel slightly tipsy.

In some Mocktails, you will find a drink called Kombucha, which is a fermented mushroom culture blended with tea. It has been used for medicinal purposes, and many claim health benefits from drinking a small amount of this brew daily. Kombucha can be purchased at most health food stores or can be home-brewed. If you don't have Kombucha, use a little sparkling soda. There is a very minor alcohol percent in Kombucha from fermentation.

Raw sake is also used in many raw cocktails, and so is organic white wines and vodka, but my virgin recipes do not include them. Feel free to indulge in a touch of raw alcohol added to any virgin Mocktail if you're so inclined.

Mockarita

SERVES 2–3

1 orange, juiced

1 teaspoon lime, juiced

1 teaspoon agave or sweetener of choice

⅛ teaspoon orange zest

1 cup soft tropical fruit, pineapple, mango, or papaya

½ cup Kombucha

¼ cup unflavored sparkling water

1 cup ice

Blend all ingredients except Kombucha, sparkling water, and ice. Blend until smooth. Add ice and blend until smooth and slushy. Pour mixture into margarita glasses, and divide Kombucha and sparkling water into glasses and stir to combine. Add a wedge of lime to the rim of the glass.

Mojito in the Raw

SERVES 1

1 spring mint

1 tablespoon lime juice

1 teaspoon agave or other sweetener

⅓ cup Kombucha

¼ cup unflavored sparkling water

Crushed ice

Choose your glasses. Crush mint and lime juice in the bottom of the glasses. Add 1 teaspoon of agave, and pour in Kombucha, sparkling water, and stir until combined. Taste for sweetness and add more if necessary. Add crushed ice if desired.

Very Dirty Mocktini

Sangria Tease

ADJUST TO AMOUNT OF PEOPLE YOU ARE SERVING.

You will need a large container with a lid as the sangria is best resting overnight in the refrigerator.

Cranberries, pomegranate, grapes, or strawberries can be used for the base of the sangria. Juice or blend any or all fruits suggested. Allow 1½ cup per person. If blending, add water to the blender to keep fruit liquid a smooth texture.

Pour the juice mixture into a large container.

Add 1 cup freshly squeezed orange juice	⅓ cup grapes
1 orange, sliced	1 kiwi, sliced
1 apple, sliced	1 bottle Kombucha
1 lemon, sliced	1 cup unflavored sparkling soda
1 lime, sliced	Agave or other sweetener to taste
½ cup strawberries	

Let rest overnight, then add more Kombucha, or more sweeteners if necessary.

Serve in a wide-mouth pitcher or a punch bowl. Add lots of ice and a ladle so fruit can be placed in glass with sangria.

Very Dirty Mocktini

SERVES 1

4 oz. cranberry juice, freshly juiced, or berries blended with water in blender	Sweetener to taste
2 oz. pineapple juice, freshly juiced or blended with water in blender	2–3 tablespoons, sparkling soda water
1 tablespoon lemon juice	Ice

Pour all ingredients except sparkling water into cocktail shaker with ice. Shake and strain into highball glasses. Add sparkling water and stir. Garnish glass with a slice of lemon.

Da Da Daiquiri

SERVES 1

Juice from 1 lime	1 tablespoon agave or sweetener of choice
1 cup strawberries	A few mint leaves
1 cup orange juice, freshly squeezed	Ice

Blend all ingredients except ice in a blender. Pour into ice-filled jar with a lid and shake several times. Pour into glass through a strainer. Garnish with a piece of orange on a skewer.

Pretender Mai Tai

SERVES 1

½ cup pineapple, freshly juiced

½ cup orange juice, freshly squeezed

½ cup coconut water

1 drop almond extract

Ice

¼ cup pomegranate juice, mixed with sweetener to make a syrup

Place all ingredients into a tall glass and stir. Use a long straw and a mint leaf to garnish

Shots

I love giving my guest shots when they arrive at our home. I juice ahead and put them in old liquor or wine bottles. These little taste treats are just enough to excite the palate.

POMEGRANATE SHOT

The easiest and cleanest way to open a pomegranate is to fill a large bowl with water, place the pomegranate in the water, and cut in half then into quarters. With pieces underwater, use your fingers to loosen the seeds. They will come out easily and sink to the bottom, and the white membrane will float to the top. Discard membrane and any outer skin, and strain out the seeds. The juicer I use, Omega 8006, juices the seeds, but if yours does not have that capacity, juice by placing seeds in your blender at lowest speed for a few moments just enough to break the juice from the seeds; if necessary, add a tablespoon of water. You don't want to grind the seed more than necessary. Use a filter nut bag or cheesecloth to strain juice.

KOMBUCHA SHOT

Shot of flavored Kombucha, purchased at your health food store.

PINEAPPLE SHOT

Pineapple juice with a touch of coconut water

GOGI BERRY WATER SHOT

Soak 1 cup gogi berries with 1 cup water. Let rest in refrigerator overnight. Strain and serve with a dash of agave and a squeeze of lime. Remaining gogi berries can be used in smoothies

TOMATO SHOT

Blend fresh tomato with a dash of tamari and tiny pinch of chili flake or jalapeño, Strain and serve cold with a grind of salt and pepper and a squeeze of lime.

LEMON GINGER SHOT

Juice lemons, add crushed ginger, to taste, a dash of water, and agave or sweetener of choice.

CRANBERRY SHOT

Blend fresh cranberries and water, strain, add sweetener of choice a squeeze of lemon, and serve cold.

GRAPE SHOT

Blend grapes of any color, strain, add a dash of carbonated water, and serve ice-cold with a touch of sweetener of choice.

PICK-ME-UP SHOT

Serve a shot of wheatgrass, followed by a shot of pomegranate or cranberry juice, and end with a shot of pineapple juice. Let the party begin!

Banana Blueberry Pancake

CHAPTER 6

breakfasts, BREADS, *and* CRACKERS

Banana Blueberry Pancake

Recipe inspired by a frozen dessert of Stacy Stowers.

MAKES 3–4 PANCAKES

2 ripe bananas

1 tablespoons agave

½ teaspoon cinnamon

¼ cup pecans chopped

½ cup blueberries

Place bananas in a bowl and gently mash with a fork until large pieces are broken down, but don't make it mushy like baby food. Add remaining ingredients, reserving ½ of the blueberries. Lightly incorporate ingredients.

Use a nonstick dehydrator sheet and divide mixture into 3–4 pancakes. Divide remaining blueberries and press into top of pancakes. Dehydrate for 4 hours at 110 degrees. When dry enough to turn, flip onto mesh screen and use a knife to help separate the pancake from the nonstick sheet if necessary. Dehydrate for another 3–4 hours. Pancakes should be soft inside, with a light crust on the outside.

TO SERVE

Serve warm right from the dehydrator with
fresh strawberries and drizzle with agave or maple syrup.

Granola Cereal or Bar

Although there are a number of ingredients and soaking must be done overnight, the assembly time is quick.

½ cup oat groats, *soaked* for 4 hours or overnight

½ cup buckwheat groats, *soaked* for 4 hours or overnight

1 cup almonds, *soaked* for 4 hours

1 cup sunflower seeds, *soaked* for 2 hours

1 cup pumpkin seeds, *soaked* for 2 hours

1 cup pecans, *soaked* for 2 hours

1½ cups dates, *soaked* for 1 hour or until soft

1 cup raisins, *soaked* for 1 hour

4 apples, coarsely chopped

½ cup blueberries

1 teaspoon cinnamon

1 tablespoon lemon juice

½ cup agave, or sweetener of choice (slightly more if making bars)

1 teaspoon maple extract

Pinch of salt

Add groats, nuts, and seeds to food processor and pulse-chop 4–5 times, stopping to scrape down sides. Remove mixture and place in a mixing bowl. Add apples, dates, agave, maple extract, lemon, cinnamon, and salt to food processor and blend until smooth. Remove to mixing bowl and blend and add blueberries and raisins. Mix until well incorporated.

Spread mixture on a nonstick dehydrator sheet and dehydrate at 110 for 8 hours. Flip over onto dehydrator screen and continue dehydrating for another 8 hours or until granola is dry. Test by breaking off a small piece to see if it's crisp.

Store in refrigerator in airtight container.

Hearty Breakfast

SERVES 2

2 apples, cored

2 tablespoons almond butter

1 banana

1 teaspoon lemon

Fresh berries

Place all ingredients in a food processor except berries and pulse-chop to break down apples. Small pieces are what you are looking for, not applesauce.

TO SERVE

Divide into bowls and put a handful of fresh berries on top.
If desired, add nuts, ground flaxseeds, or hemp seeds.

Sprouted Oat Groats

SERVES 1-2

1 cup oat groats, sprouted (see sprouting instructions on p. 115)

Almond milk (see recipe on p. 74)

½ banana

½ cup berries

1 tablespoons raisin

2 tablespoons chopped nuts of your choice

Place oat groats in a glass jar with a lid and 2 cups filtered water. Place in dehydrator at 105–110 degrees and dehydrate overnight. Drain water from groats and rinse.

TO SERVE

Place groats in a bowl and add fruit and milk. Add sweetener of choice if desired.
Sprinkle with ground flaxseeds.

Rawkin Cereal

SERVES 1

¼ cup oat groats, soaked overnight

½ cup almonds, soaked overnight and drained

2 tablespoon hemp seeds

¼ cup sunflower seeds

½ cup fruit of choice, chopped

Sprinkle of cinnamon

2 chopped dates or 1 tablespoon raisins

Almond milk (see recipe on p. 74)

Place oat groats in a glass jar with a lid along and 2 cups filtered water. Place in dehydrator at 105–110 degrees and dehydrate overnight. Groats will soften and be ready to eat in the morning.

Place all ingredients except milk in a bowl and mix well.

TO SERVE

Add almond milk and berries or fruit of choice and enjoy.

Bread and Cracker Recipes

Bread seems to be a food missed when beginning a raw food journey. Learning to make raw breads and crackers will satisfy cravings and help you stay on the path.

Bagels

MAKES 6 BAGELS

Surprised? And no, they are not quite like New York bagels. However, when adding all the traditional toppings, it truly is a satisfying alternative.

In place of smoked salmon, I use kombu seaweed. Kombu is slightly salty like the sea and softens when soaked overnight in water. Add cashew nut cream cheese, sliced tomato, red onion, and capers and one would think they just had a nice New York deli breakfast.

The ingredients list is long, but the ingredients go together quickly, making bagels quite easy to prepare.

2 cups sprouted wheatberry, ground in blender, spice or coffee grinder

½ cup sunflower seeds, ground in blender, spice or coffee grinder

¼ cup agave or sweetener of choice

1¾ cup zucchini, coarsely chopped

3 tablespoons extra-virgin olive oil

2 tablespoons sunflower lecithin

1 apple, coarsely chopped

3 tablespoons nutritional yeast (not raw but vegan)

½ cup sun-dried tomatoes, soaked until soft, approximately 1 hour

1 tablespoon lemon juice

½ teaspoon salt

½ cup onion, chopped

1 avocado, chopped

¼ cup Irish moss paste (see recipe on pg. 50)

½ cup flaxseed, ground into a meal in spice or coffee grinder

½ cup or more filtered water as needed

Place all ingredients except flax meal in food processor; grind until ingredients are broken down and fluffy. Best done in two batches. When all ingredients are well incorporated and the mixture looks light, remove half and add flax meal to the remaining half and pulse until flax is incorporated. Place dough in a bowl and, using your hands, blend.

Drop 2–3 good tablespoons of dough onto a nonstick dehydrator sheet and shape by hand to look like a bagel that has been cut in half about ½-inch thick or more. If desired, use a round cookie cutter or glass to make shapes uniform. Make a hole in the center with your finger. What's a bagel without a hole? Use the flat side of large knife or spatula to smooth around the outside edges.

Dehydrate for 2–3 hours at 105–110 degrees. Flip bagels by placing another mesh dehydrator tray on top and invert so that your original sheet of bagels is upside down, which will allow you to peel off the nonstick sheet. Continue to dehydrate for approximately 8 hours or longer, or until bagel feels light. Look for a crusty outside and slightly soft in the center.

TO SERVE

Top your bagel with cream cheese (see recipe on page 144), soaked kombu torn in strips, a slice of tomato, a thin slice of red onion, and a sprinkle of capers.

Caramelized Onion Bread

MAKES 16–18 SLICES

3 cups onion, thinly sliced

2 cups sprouted wheatberry, ground in blender, spice or coffee grinder

1 cup sunflower seeds, ground in blender, spice or coffee grinder

¼ cup agave or sweetener of choice

2 cups zucchini, coarsely chopped

3 tablespoons extra-virgin olive oil

2 tablespoons sunflower lecithin

1 apple, coarsely chopped

3 tablespoons nutritional yeast (not raw but vegan)

1 cup sun-dried tomatoes, soaked until soft

1 tablespoon lemon juice

1 clove garlic

½ teaspoon salt

1 avocado, chopped

¼ cup Irish moss paste (see recipe on p. 50)

1 cup flaxseed, ground into a meal in your spice or coffee grinder

½ cup or more of water as needed

1 teaspoon oregano

1 teaspoon thyme

½ cup soaked dates

2 tablespoons tamari, nama shoyu, or Bragg's

Freshly milled pepper to taste

Sprinkle onions with salt, Stevia, or dry sweetener of choice and let sit for 30 minutes.

Drain dates, pit and place in a high-speed blender with 1 tablespoon tamari, 1 tablespoon water, and a dash of extra-virgin olive oil.

Add the date mixture to the onions and mix well. Place onions on a nonstick dehydrator sheet and dehydrate for 2 hours or until soft.

Place all remaining ingredients except onion and flax meal in food processor. Grind until ingredients are broken down and fluffy. Best done in two batches. When all ingredients are well incorporated and the mixture looks light, remove half and add flax meal to the remaining half. Pulse until flax is incorporated. Place all the dough in mixing bowl, add caramelized onions, and use hands to incorporate.

Spread dough onto two nonstick dehydrator sheets, about ½-inch thick.

Dehydrate for 8 hours at 105–110 degrees. When dry on top, flip onto mesh dehydrator tray and invert. Peel off nonstick sheet and continue to dehydrate for approximately 8–10 hours or more until bread feels light and crusty on the outside and slightly soft in the center.

Tip { I see an ALT sandwich in your future (avocado, lettuce, and tomato).

Cornbread

2 cups fresh corn kernels

1 red bell pepper, chopped

2 tablespoons onion, chopped

1 medium tomato, chopped

1 teaspoon extra-virgin olive oil

½ teaspoon turmeric

½ teaspoon oregano

3 tablespoons onion

1 clove garlic, minced

¼ cup carrot, chopped

¼ teaspoon paprika

⅛ teaspoon Himalayan or Celtic sea salt

Freshly milled pepper

½ cup sunflower seeds, ground in spice or coffee grinder

¼ cup flaxseed, ground in spice or coffee grinder

To spice up, add a piece of jalapeño pepper

In your food processor, place all ingredients except ¼ cup corn and ground sunflower and flax meal. Pulse-chop until well incorporated.

Place mixture in a bowl, add corn and flax meal, and mix well.

Spread on nonstick dehydrator sheet into squares about ½–1-inch thick. Dehydrate at 115 for 6–8 hours, then flip over to mesh tray. Dehydrate another 6–8 or until desired texture. If cornbread is too soft to flip to mesh trap, dehydrate longer until you can.

Tip { Makes a great side to Sprouted Chili (see recipe on page 174).

Herbed Bread

MAKES 9 SLICES

2 cups sprouted wheatberries, or kamut

2 cups zucchini, chopped

4 pulps from 4 juiced carrots

¼ cup pumpkin seeds, ground in spice or coffee grinder

¼ cup sunflower seeds, ground in spice or coffee grinder

½ cup sun-dried tomatoes, soaked until soft

1 tablespoon extra-virgin olive oil

Pinch of Himalayan or Celtic salt and freshly milled pepper

1 tablespoon mixed marjoram, oregano, rosemary, basil

Place all ingredients except flax meal in the food processor and process until smooth as possible, stopping to scrape down the sides when necessary.

Remove from processor and place mixture in a bowl. Add flax meal and combine well.

Spread mixture into a large square on nonstick dehydrator sheet. Dehydrate at 110 degrees for 6 hours. Flip onto mesh tray, score for 9 slices, and dehydrate an additional 6–8 hours. Finished bread should be light and crusty on the outside and moist on the inside.

Sweet or Savory Bread

This bread is dense and delicious for breakfast with raw almond butter and banana.

I discovered this bread by accident when I had sprouted wheatberries that needed to be used. I was out of zucchini and other ingredients I use in my breads, but this is now one of my favorite treats.

2 cups sprouted wheatberries

½ cup pecans, chopped

1 apple, diced

¼ cup sunflower seeds

¼ cup raisins soaked

¼ cup hemp seeds

1 teaspoon cinnamon

¼ cup flax meal (flaxseeds ground in spice grinder)

¼ cup extra-virgin olive oil

⅛ teaspoon Himalayan or Celtic sea salt

Place wheatberries in a food processor with olive oil and salt. Blend until smooth. Scrape down the sides and add remainder of ingredients except raisins, pulse 4–5 times, and leave some chunk. Mix raisins in by hand.

Divide mixture into thirds onto a nonstick dehydrator sheet. Press down to make ½ inch thick. Score with spatula. Dehydrate 4 hours at 110 degrees, then flip onto mesh tray and dehydrate another 6 hours or until crusty on the outside and soft in center.

Tip { Add herbs and raw olives, omit raisins, and enjoy savory bread.

Mediterranean Flat Bread

3 cups sprouted buckwheat or wheatberries, ground in blender or coffee grinder

¼ cup sunflower seeds, ground in your blender or coffee grinder

¼ cup agave or sweetener of choice

½ zucchini, chopped

3 tablespoons lecithin (an emulsifier, not raw but vegan)

6 tablespoons olive oil

2 teaspoons Celtic or Himalayan sea salt

3–4 tablespoons Italian seasoning, rosemary, thyme, basil, marjoram, oregano

2 cloves garlic, chopped

2 cups spring water

¾ cup nutritional yeast (not raw but vegan)

2 cups sun-dried tomatoes, soaked for 20 minutes to 1 hour

2 cups flax (ground in clean coffee grinder)

In food processor, place all ingredients except nutritional yeast, sun-dried tomatoes, and ground flaxseed. Process until well incorporated. Add sun-dried tomatoes and pulse-chop until smooth. If mixture is too thick to add flax at this point, remove from processor into a bowl and mix in ground flax by hand. If mixture is not too thick, add flaxseed and pulse-chop until well incorporated.

Divide mixture in half and place onto 2 nonstick dehydrator sheets. Shape into large squares, ½ inch to ¾ inch thick. Brush top with extra-virgin olive oil. Dehydrate for approximately 10 hours at 105–110 degrees. When dry on top, flip onto mesh screen and cut into desired size. Dehydrate for another 9 hours or until crusty on the outside and slightly soft in the middle.

Toppings

This is a good time to use your creativity and make one of your favorite pizza toppings, or tapenades (see pages 146, 149).

Flaxseed Crackers

2 cups flaxseed, ½ cup soaked in 2 cups of water for 4 hours or until they become gelatinous and 1½ cup ground into a meal

1 cup sunflower seeds, soak half the seeds in water for 4 hours and grind the other half into a meal

¼ cup sun-dried tomatoes, soaked until soft

2 tablespoons chopped onion

2 tablespoons tamari, nama shoyu, or Bragg's

1 tablespoon herbs, Italian, Herbs de Provence, or any of your favorites

½ teaspoon Himalayan or Celtic sea salt, or more to taste

In food processor, mix all ingredients but the soaked flax and sunflower seeds. When well blended, place the mixture in a bowl and add the soaked seeds, mixing well to incorporate.

Spread on nonstick dehydrator sheet. If sticky, wet your spatula to help make it easier to spread. Don't worry if there is a hole or two, just try to make them flat and thin so they dry evenly. Use a flat-edged spatula to score into crackers' size desired. Scoring will make it easier to break when dry.

Dehydrate 7–8 hours. Flip over to the mesh dehydrator tray and dry 7 more hours or until crisp.

Tip { For a sweeter cracker, leave out the onion, tamari, and herbs. Add raisins, sweetener, and cinnamon.

Pizza Crackers

Soaking and dehydrating is the only time this recipe takes. The actual prep time is 20 minutes or less. Take out all you ingredients before starting and place them on your workspace. You will need a food processor, a grinder for your seeds (sometimes a blender works), a spatula, a bowl for soaking nuts and one for tomatoes, a chopping knife, and a dehydrator.

2 cups flaxseeds soaked in 2 cups of water 4–6 hours

¼ cup sun-dried tomatoes, soaked until soft

¼ cup of hemp seeds

¼ cup sunflower seeds, ground in a spice or coffee grinder

¼ cup pumpkin seeds, ground in a spice or coffee grinder

½ cup onion, chopped

1 small clove garlic, crushed

1 teaspoon extra-virgin olive oil

Dash of tamari, nama shoyu, or Bragg's

1 teaspoon lemon juice

1 tablespoon Italian seasonings, oregano, rosemary, marjoram, basil

Himalayan or Celtic sea salt to taste

Freshly milled pepper to taste

¼ cup raw olives, finely chopped

Water as needed

In food processor, chop all ingredients except olives until smooth. Adjust salt and herbs to taste. Scrape down the sides and add water if needed to smooth out any lumps. Mix in olives by hand.

Divide onto 2–3 nonstick dehydrator sheets and spread into large squares about ¹⁄₁₆ inch thick. Dehydrate for 6 hours at 105 degrees, then flip and score. Dehydrate another 6 hours or until crisp and dry.

Corn Chips

6–8 ears corn, kernels cut from the cob

½ cup ground golden flaxseed (ground in a spice or clean coffee grinder)

¼ cup onion, chopped

⅛ teaspoon salt

¼ teaspoon combined Mexican seasonings, such as cumin, oregano, and garlic powder

In your food processor, mix corn, onion, and salt. Process until on the smooth side. Add ground flax and pulse to blend.

Spread thin with a rubber spatula on nonstick dehydrator sheet. Wet the back of spatula and smooth mixture out evenly. Pick up tray and lightly tap it down on the countertop, turning and tapping to aid in spreading mixture. Mixture can also be dropped by tablespoons onto nonstick sheet to create little rounds a bit thicker. Dehydrate for 24 hours or until dry and crispy. Flip onto mesh tray halfway through dehydrating and cut into desired chip size.

Tip { Score after spreading on nonstick dehydrator sheet or before flipping, use kitchen scissors to cut into desired size.

Gazpacho Soup

CHAPTER 7

Soups

Butternut Squash Soup

SERVES 2–4

3 cups almond milk

3 cups butternut squash, cut into chunks

1 tablespoon onion

½ stalk celery, cut into chunks

1 carrot, chopped

1 tablespoon agave or sweetener of choice

⅛ teaspoon curry powder

⅛ teaspoon cumin

Dash of cinnamon

1 clove garlic

Dash or two tamari

Himalayan or Celtic sea salt

Freshly milled pepper to taste

Place all ingredients in a high-powered blender and blend until smooth. To warm soup, place in dehydrator, a double boiler, or in a pot and gently warm. Stir constantly and be careful not to overheat.

TO SERVE
Divide in bowl and top with sour cream (see recipe on page 146). Sprinkle with chives or green onions.

Broccoli Soup

SERVES 2–3

2 cups almond or cashew milk (see recipe on p. 74)

2 cups broccoli, broken into florets

1 avocado, cut in chunks

1 tablespoon onion

1 clove garlic

½ stalk celery, coarsely chopped

1 tablespoon extra-virgin olive oil

½ teaspoon cumin

Himalayan or Celtic sea salt to taste

Freshly milled pepper to taste

Place all ingredients into a high-powered blender and blend until smooth. Refrigerate for 2 hours to meld ingredients. Warm in dehydrator, double boiler, or a pot on the stove, stirring constantly. Do not overheat to retain the enzymes. Warm as in baby-bottle warm.

TO SERVE
Divide into bowls and top with sour cream. (See recipe on page 146.) Garnish with vegetable slice, if desired.

Tom Yum Miso Soup

SERVES 2–4

2 cups coconut water form fresh from young Thai coconuts, when possible (Water can also be purchased in a box from health food store or Asian markets, but to my liking, not as tasty)

1 cup spring water

1 heaping tablespoon light miso, unprocessed if possible

½ lime, juiced

1" piece ginger

2 cloves garlic

3 green onions (scallions), chopped

½ cup spinach, coarsely chopped

¼ cup cilantro, leaves only

1 stalk lemongrass, lower part, chopped

4 kaffir lime leaves

2 shitake mushrooms, thinly sliced

Blend coconut water, springwater, miso, lime, ginger, and garlic until smooth.

Pour liquid base in a pan and add remaining ingredients. Warm lightly so as not to overheat. Turn the flame off and let it sit 10 minutes to meld tastes. Warm again and serve, removing kaffir lime leaves and lemongrass. Be sure not to overheat soup and "cook" the ingredients. Keep it raw.

If desired, you may add ½ cup coconut meat to the blender with the coconut water to make soup thicker.

There is no replacement for the taste kaffir lime leaves and lemongrass stalk add to this soup. These items can be purchased at Asian markets. The soup is still tasty without these items, but it is definitely superb and sublime with them.

TO SERVE
Ladle into bowls and garnish with chopped cilantro or more chopped green onion.

Tip { Add some spiralized peeled zucchini noodles or raw sushi rice.

Corn Soup

SERVES 2–3

3 cups almond milk

4 cups fresh corn, cut from the cob

1 avocado

1 tablespoon onion

1 teaspoon cumin

⅛ teaspoon turmeric

Himalayan or Celtic sea salt

Freshly milled pepper

In a high-powered blender, combine all ingredients, reserving ½ cup of corn. Blend until smooth. Taste for seasonings and adjust if necessary.

TO SERVE
Divide soup between bowls and place remaining corn kernels in each bowl. Garnish with chopped cilantro or parsley. May be warmed in dehydrator, double boiler, or in a pot, being careful to not overheat and just make it warm.

Thick Tomato Soup

SERVES 2–3

7 medium tomatoes, heirloom if possible

½ cup sun-dried tomatoes, soaked in filtered water until soft

1 avocado

1 tablespoon onion, coarsely chopped

1 small clove garlic, coarsely chopped

2 tablespoons basil, coarsely chopped

Himalayan or Celtic sea salt

Freshly milled pepper

Water as needed

In a food processor, add all ingredients and pulse-chop until incorporated and slightly chunky or to your liking. Add water to obtain desired texture.

Pour into a jar or bowl and warm in dehydrator, a double boiler, or gently heat on stove just until warm. Do not overheat.

Cream of Mushroom Soup

SERVES 2

2 cups mushrooms

2 tablespoons extra-virgin olive oil

2 tablespoons tamari, namya shoyu or Bragg's

Vegetable broth (recipe follows)

2 cups cashew milk

1 tomato

1 cup sun-dried tomatoes, soaked in water until soft

1 date

Salt and pepper to taste

Himalayan or celtic sea salt

Freshly milled pepper

Wipe mushroom caps with a damp cloth. Destem and slice. Marinate mushrooms and stems in olive oil and coconut aminos or tamari for 30 minutes.

For the vegetable broth

1 zucchini, finely chopped

¼ medium onion, finely chopped

2 stalks celery, finely chopped

2 carrot, peeled and finely chopped

½ cup parsnip, peeled and finely chopped

Small piece of broccoli

¼ piece of sweet potato

½ teaspoon poultry seasoning

½ teaspoon oregano, bay leaf, or other seasoning of choice

3 cups filtered water

Put zucchini, onion, celery, carrot, broccoli, sweet potato, and seasonings in a pot and cover with water.

Warm the mixture. (Take care to not cook or overheat.) Taste for seasonings and adjust to your liking. Remove warm pot from stove and cover. Let rest until vegetables soften, about 30 minutes. This may also be done in the dehydrator.

To blender, add vegetable broth, cashew milk, tomato, sun-dried tomatoes, including soaking water, date, salt and pepper, and blend until smooth.

Add ¾ of the mushrooms to blender including marinade liquid and blend until smooth.

Add water if necessary to make a smooth thick texture or more cashews to make it thicker. Taste and adjust seasonings.

Put soup back in pot and warm, stirring constantly so as not to overheat and destroy enzymes, or place in glass jar with lid and warm in dehydrator.

Divide balance of mushrooms into each bowl, ladle in soup mixture, and garnish with chopped chives.

Gazpacho

Gazpacho is widely consumed throughout Spain and Portugal. Gazpacho is high in nutrients and low in calories. For me, gazpacho is the taste of summer.

When I lived in Taos, New Mexico, people would ask me what I grew in my garden, and I would answer gazpacho! The ingredients are simple and easy to grow and include tomatoes, cucumbers, sweet bell peppers, garlic, and onion. During the summer months, I could eat gazpacho daily, especially made with heirloom tomatoes. If you've never tasted cold soup before, then gazpacho is the one to try.

Gazpacho makes a satisfying lunch or a starter for a more elaborate meal. I like to make this soup a day ahead to allow the flavors to meld together to give it extra flavor.

3 cups ripe red tomatoes, seeded and diced (heirloom whenever possible)

½ cup celery, diced

1 avocado, diced

2 cups cucumber, diced

2 cups red bell pepper, diced

1 red onion, diced

¼ cup basil, chopped

1 teaspoon garlic, minced

1 teaspoon cumin

Pinch of cayenne, if you like it spicy

Salt and pepper to taste

1 tablespoon juice from a lemon or lime

1 teaspoon apple cider vinegar

2 cups of veggie juice—made by juicing a combination of any vegetables you have on hand including celery, carrots, broccoli, tomato, leek, cilantro, spinach, and red bell pepper. You can also make this juice in your blender by adding water to the mixture.

Mix together diced tomato, celery, avocado, cucumber, red pepper, and onion. Divide the mixture in half, placing ½ into your blender along with the garlic, cumin, cayenne, salt and pepper, lemon juice, and vinegar. Blend until smooth. Add vegetable juice to the blender and blend until incorporated.

Taste for seasonings and adjust to your liking. Pour the mixture into the bowl of diced vegetables and store covered in the refrigerator. Let sit overnight, or at least 3–4 hours if you just can't wait.

Spice it up a bit with jalapeño or dried red chili flakes. You can serve in shot glasses with a wedge of lime for a dinner starter; or for a lunch portion, ladle into large colorful bowls and garnish with cilantro leaves and a thin wedge of lime.

Tips {

Serve with a side bowl of chopped tomatoes, cucumber, red onion, avocado, and red chili peppers for guests to add more chunks or spice to their soup.

Avocado Soup

SERVES 4

1 garlic clove, minced

1" piece of fresh ginger, peeled and minced, or ⅛ teaspoon powdered ginger

⅛ teaspoon cumin

1 small piece of jalapeño, seeded (or more if you like it spicy)

2 tablespoons extra-virgin olive oil

Juice from 5 stalks celery, 1 large cucumber, 1 red bell pepper, and ¼ of a medium mild onion; Add water to equal 4 cups

3 avocados, chopped

Juice of 1 lime

Salt and pepper to taste

Sour cream (see recipe on p. 146)

½ cup cilantro, chopped

⅛ teaspoon coriander

Place all ingredients in blender, reserving, sour cream, cilantro, and coriander, and blend well. Taste to adjust seasonings. Place in a closed container in the refrigerator to chill for 30 minutes.

Pour into 4 bowls, top with sour cream, chopped cilantro, and a sprinkle of coriander.

CHAPTER 8

salads

AND

DRESSINGS

How to Sprout

Sprouting is like having an indoor garden all year round. Sprouts are packed with energy-giving nutrients, enzymes, and vitamins. Sprouting is very inexpensive. You can grow pounds of greens for pennies in your own kitchen.

Sprouts and microgreens can be grown indoors all year round. They are easy to grow and are packed with nutrients and taste very delicious. Enjoy a wonderful live high-protein salad right from your own kitchen garden.

Sprouts are easy to grow. All you need is a glass jar, seeds, and water. Add sprouts to salads, sandwiches, soups, and juices. Sprouting seeds and containers can be purchased by mail. (See suppliers on page 52.)

Use a wide-mouth canning jar with a piece of cheesecloth and a rubber band or a mesh screen in the screw top of the jar, or purchase a seed-sprouting tray. (See suppliers on page 52.)

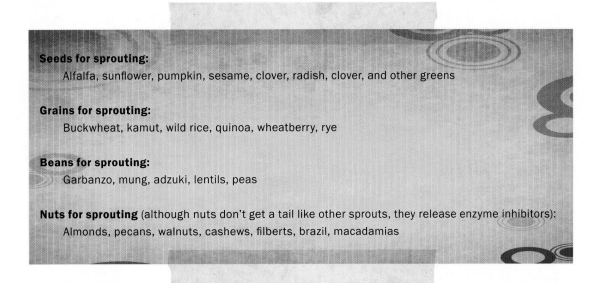

Seeds for sprouting:
   Alfalfa, sunflower, pumpkin, sesame, clover, radish, clover, and other greens

Grains for sprouting:
   Buckwheat, kamut, wild rice, quinoa, wheatberry, rye

Beans for sprouting:
   Garbanzo, mung, adzuki, lentils, peas

Nuts for sprouting (although nuts don't get a tail like other sprouts, they release enzyme inhibitors):
   Almonds, pecans, walnuts, cashews, filberts, brazil, macadamias

General method for sprouting seeds: Rinse and drain seeds. Place 3 tablespoons of seeds in your sprouting container. Add filtered water to cover 3 inches above seeds. Leave overnight in a dark, cool place. Next morning, cover the top of the jar with cheesecloth and fasten with a rubber band. The cheesecloth will act as a strainer. Turn the jar over and drain out the soaking water. Use soaking water for smoothies if desired. Remove all water from the jar and rinse the seeds two more times with filtered water. Seeds will rot if water is left in the jar. I like to turn the jar over and stand it cheesecloth-side down in a bowl to keep any water from staying inside the jar. Store in a dark, cool place. That evening, rinse the seeds twice again and stand the jar on end in the bowl. If you are around during the day, you can rinse a third time. Seeds need to be rinsed at least twice a day. Continue to rinse daily and check in 3–4 days to see if little "tails" are showing. Most seeds will be ready to harvest in 5 days. Drain and shake out all the water. Store sprouts in the refrigerator in an airtight container for about a week.

Grain sprouting is a little different as no tail appears. Wild rice will split open and other grains will just soften. Simply place grains in a jar and fill with filtered water 4 inches above the grains. Place in dehydrator at 105 degrees for 12 to 24 hours. Drain, rinse, and use. If you don't have a dehydrator, place in a warm place like on top of your oven or wrapped in a towel outside during summer months. Be sure to rinse and drain well.

Salads

It was difficult deciding which recipes to include in this section as I literally have hundreds of salad combinations to choose from. Just like incorporating juicing or smoothies on a daily basis, I feel salads are imperative to maintaining a vibrant lifestyle.

Salads were once considered a starter to a meal, and in France, it was said to be best for digestion served after a meal. Others have said the French serve the salad last because the vinegar in the salad dressing destroyed the taste of the wine.

Salads in one form or another date back to the fourteenth century and were enjoyed by the ancient Romans and Greeks. Today, we eat salads as a main course for both lunch and dinner.

Depending on the season and where in the country you live, fresh salad fixings can be grown in your own backyard, in pots, or on a windowsill. They can be purchased from farmers markets or a local grower in some cities year round. If you can't find greens because you live in winter climates, I highly recommend sprouting.

Did you ever think of eating raw parsnip? What about eating raw beets or sweet potato? If you haven't tried these, all I can say is you are in for a treat. Even if you don't care for these vegetables cooked, I think you will discover a completely different and delicate taste when they are eaten raw.

Those of us who have adopted a raw food lifestyle do not live on salads alone, but I think I could with the generous selection of unique vegetables. Every day is a new surprise. Living in California makes it easy to eat salads all year round, and in summer there is an abundance of colorful and inviting vegetables, including a wide variety of dark leafy greens. Salads are quick and easy to make and full of nourishing vitamins. With some basic ingredients and great salad dressings, I never seem to be at a loss to create a delicious meal.

When I first started eating raw foods, I wanted more elaborate dishes. After a short time though, all I craved were dark leafy green salads. Greens make my body feel fantastic.

I prefer to eat salads at home because I favor eating organic food. However, when traveling, unless I find a raw food or organic restaurant, salads are the only place I look on a standard restaurant menu. I can usually find some acceptable combination by leaving off foods that are not vegan and raw and adding foods that are. I find most restaurants very accommodating.

lettuce

Lettuce is best when very cold. Wash selected lettuce and wrap in a paper towel or clean kitchen towel and refrigerate until ready to use, or wash the lettuce in a bowl of springwater, dry in a salad spinner, and wrap in a paper or kitchen towel and refrigerate until crisp and cold. Lettuce accepts dressing better when leaves are completely dry.

Chilling the serving plates 10–15 minutes or more in your freezer ensures the salad will be served nice and cold.

Microgreen Salad

Microgreens are one of my favorite live foods. They are a mixture of lettuce and herbs that are harvested when young and very tiny. Microgreens have about an inch-long stem, longer than most sprouts. They are easy to grow with a pre-packaged seed mix either outdoors in a flat, or inside on a sunny windowsill. My personal favorite is a Mesclun mix. Many health food stores and specialty grocery stores carry microgreens already sprouted. (See page 52 to learn where to purchase seeds for sprouting.)

Place desired amount of microgreens in a salad bowl. Drizzle on extra-virgin olive oil, and squeeze on a generous amount of lemon juice. Add a few grinds of sea salt and lightly toss.

Caesar Salad

SERVES 4

From Italy to Tijuana, Mexico, there are many claims from around the globe as to who invented the Caesar salad. Caesar Cardini was born in Lago Maggiore, Italy. He emigrated to the US and eventually opened a restaurant in Tijuana, Mexico. The salad dates back to around 1927. The originator controversy still exists. Is Caesar Cardini the one who invented the salad, or was it another family member . . . or, was it actually someone in Italy? I don't think we will ever really know the answer, but many articles claim the Caesar salad was invented in Tijuana, Mexico.

I grew up eating Cardini salad dressing that my mother bought in a bottle. And years later, I had many Caesar salads at the original Caesar's Restaurant in Tijuana made right at our table by a gentleman in a very shiny suit. I was allowed to write down the recipe, and original or not, it was fantastic. Of course, I now enjoy the raw version I adapted from the original recipe, and I'm very happy with the outcome. It's simply delicious. For added elegance, put your serving plates in the freezer to chill.

For the Salad

Use inner hearts of 3 heads of romaine lettuce and save the softer outer leaves for a different salad or juicing. Wash and wrap the leaves in paper or kitchen towel and place in fridge to crisp and dry.

For the Dressing

In a small mixing bowl, whisk together the following:

2 garlic cloves, crushed

½ cup extra-virgin olive oil

⅛ teaspoon tamari

1 teaspoon capers, well mashed

1 lemon or lime, juiced (key limes are in the original recipe)

⅛ teaspoon Dijon mustard, or homemade mustard (See recipe on p. 61)

Himalayan salt and pepper to taste

Freshly milled black pepper to taste

¼ cup Parmesan cheese (see recipe on p. 146)

For the Croutons (Optional)

1 small tomato, cut in half

½ sweet red pepper, cut in half

3 cloves garlic, cut in half

¼ cup olive oil

½ tablespoon capers

¼ teaspoon Himalayan sea salt

½ jicama, peeled, cut in wide strips, and then cut into crouton-size squares

Place all ingredients except the jicama in your blender and blend until well incorporated.

Tips { A mandolin slicer will quickly slice the jicama.

Marinate the jicama squares in the mixture for 1–2 hours. Place jicama squares on nonstick dehydrator sheet and dehydrate 8–12 hours at 110 degrees. Turn directly onto mesh tray and dehydrate another 3 hours. Taste for desired texture.

TO ASSEMBLE

Place whole crisp dry romaine lettuce in a wooden bowl.

> Slowly add ½ of the dressing.
> Sprinkle in half the Parmesan cheese.
> Turn leaves gently with your hands to coat leaves.
> Add more dressing and turn by hand again to cover all the leaves.
> Add balance of Parmesan cheese and turn by hand again.

TO SERVE

Remove salad plates from the freezer if you chilled them, and divide the leaves between 4 plates. Sprinkle on more Parmesan cheese if desired and place 3–4 croutons on each salad.

Traditionally, this salad is eaten by hand, picking up whole leaves. I personally enjoy eating it this way.

Arugula Salad

SERVES 2

4 cups arugula
½ red bell pepper, thinly sliced

¼ cup red onion, thinly sliced

For the Dressing

1 shallot, peeled and chopped

¼ cup extra-virgin olive oil

1 tablespoon sesame seed oil

1 tablespoon apple cider vinegar

1 tablespoon white miso

1 teaspoon ginger

Place all dressing ingredients in high-powered blender and blend until smooth. Taste for seasonings and adjust if necessary.

Pour over arugula, red pepper, and onion and toss well.

Fennel Salad

SERVES 2

2 cups fennel bulb, thinly sliced

1 cup arugula or spinach, washed and dried in a salad spinner. Wrap in paper or kitchen towel and place in the refrigerator to chill and crisp.

½ red sweet pepper, thinly sliced

Parmesan cheese (see recipe on p. 146)

For the Dressing

½ cup extra-virgin olive oil

4 tablespoons lemon juice, or more to taste

1 clove garlic, minced

Himalayan salt to taste

Freshly milled pepper

Whisk all ingredients in a small mixing bowl until well incorporated.

TO SERVE

Toss salad ingredients in a large salad bowl. Add and toss ½ of the dressing and lightly toss. Add more dressing until all the leaves are lightly covered. Place on 2 chilled plates and top with a sprinkle of pine nuts and a grind of freshly milled pepper.

Sweet Pepper Antipasto

SERVES 6–7 FOR ANTIPASTO (TRANSLATED FROM ITALIAN "BEFORE THE MEAL")

For the Antipasto

1 red pepper	1 orange pepper
1 yellow pepper	raw olives

For the Marinade

3–4 tablespoons extra-virgin olive oil

A pinch each, oregano, rosemary, basil, thyme, marjoram

6 fresh basil leaves, chopped

1–2 cloves garlic, minced or crushed

1 tablespoon lemon juice

2 teaspoons capers

Himalayan salt and freshly milled pepper to taste

Thinly slice peppers. Whisk marinade to blend and toss with peppers and olives. Let rest for 3 hours or more in the refrigerator.

TO SERVE
Place peppers on a large serving platter or tray, keeping each color pepper separate. Place olives in a small bowl and set in the middle of the platter.

Tip { You can also make the same marinade for button mushrooms and raw artichoke hearts cut in chunks and put on toothpicks to add to your antipasto.

Chop-Chop Salad

For the Salad

Yellow squash	Carrot
Zucchini	Red cabbage
Asparagus	Turnip
Broccoli	Fennel bulb
String beans	Fresh whole herbs such as mint, tarragon, sorrel, and dill for garnish
Parsnip	

Chop all vegetables into small, even pieces.

For the Dressing

½ cup extra-virgin olive oil	¼ cup coconut aminos or tamari
½ cup tahini	Himalayan salt to taste
¼ bunch of fresh parsley	Freshly milled pepper
¼ cup apple cider vinegar	2–3 tablespoons agave or sweetener of choice
⅓ cup cashews	¾ cup more or less water, added slowly while blending
3–4 tablespoons lemon juice	
2 cloves garlic	

Finished dressing should be a smooth, creamy, thick pourable dressing.

Place dressing ingredients into a blender and blend until smooth.

Place all salad ingredients in a bowl and add desired amount of dressing. Some people like a small amount and others like it very wet. The vegetables hold up very well with dressing. You could also serve extra dressing on the side for each guest to add his or her own.

TO SERVE

For beautiful plating, use an empty 8 oz. can that has both top and bottom removed. Place the can in the middle of salad plate and pack the salad into the can about ½–¾ full, pressing down lightly to pack in. Slowly lift up the can while pushing the salad down with a spoon, which will leave a tall stack of salad on the plate. Garnish with a sprig of mint, a few tarragon or sorrel leaves, and a sprig of dill. Nice served chilled.

Cool Cool Cabbage Salad

Cabbage is a cruciferous vegetable. It is filled with photochemical that are believed to inhibit breast cancer. A study published in the journal Cancer Research *confirmed that women who eat more cruciferous vegetables have a much lower risk of breast cancer. Cruciferous vegetables contain antioxidant enabling our system to fight carcinogens and clean out toxins from our bodies. One cup a day provides anti-cancer benefits. Other cruciferous vegetables include brussels sprouts, cauliflower, broccoli, collard greens, kale, and bok choy.*

- 1 cup each Asian cabbage, green head cabbage and red cabbage, shredded
- 1 cup Asian pea pods, trimmed and cut into lengthwise strips
- 2 scallions, chopped
- 3 brussels sprouts, thinly sliced

- ½ cup carrots, shredded
- ½ cup bean sprouts
- ¼ cup raisins
- ½ cup cashews, chopped
- 1 tablespoon sesame seeds, black if possible

Place all ingredients except the cashews and the sesame seeds in a large bowl.

For the Dressing

2 tablespoons extra-virgin olive oil	1 heaping tablespoon raw tahini
1 tablespoon sesame seed oil	1–2 teaspoons agave or sweetener of choice
1 tablespoon apple cider vinegar	½ teaspoon or more fresh ginger, finely chopped
1 teaspoon coconut aminos, tamari, Bragg's, or nama shoyu	Pinch of Himalayan salt and freshly ground pepper to taste

Place dressing ingredients in a small mixing bowl and whisk until well blended.

Taste for seasonings and adjust.

TO ASSEMBLE
Pour dressing onto the salad mix. Gently toss until well coated. Let salad rest to absorb the dressing. If more dressing is desired, make up another small batch and add to the salad. Chill.

TO SERVE
Remove cabbage salad from the refrigerator and mix in the chopped cashews. Sprinkle the sesame seeds and garnish with ½ slice of orange. Serve with chopsticks.

Simple Mediterranean Salad

SERVES 2–3

When the warm breezes blow, and the nights are as warm as the day, this simple salad will please your palate. Always buy the freshest organic in-season produce possible. The simplicity of this salad requires the best extra-virgin olive oil you can afford.

4 firm heirloom or slightly green tomatoes, cut into wedges	1 cup raw olives, pitted
2 sweet red or yellow peppers, seeded, cored, and sliced into strips	Good-quality extra-virgin olive oil
	1–2 tablespoons lemon juice
1 small or ½ medium sweet onion or red onion, sliced into strips	Himalayan or Celtic sea salt, to taste
½ cucumber, coarsely diced	Freshly milled pepper to taste

Place the vegetables in a bowl and sprinkle generously with extra-virgin olive oil, lemon, salt, and pepper. Let salad rest for 15–20 minutes to meld flavors together.

Taste for salt and pepper and adjust if necessary. Flavors should be lemony and light.

Served chilled on lettuce leaves.

High-Energy Salad

SERVES 2

9 romaine lettuce leaves, ribbon-cut

6 dinosaur kale leaves, stems removed and ribbon-cut

1 bunch flat-leaf parsley, stems removed and leaves finely chopped

1 bunch bok choy, chopped

Handful of purslane, chopped

Handful of lamb's quarters, chopped

Handful of arugula, chopped

¼ cup dill, chopped

½ cup basil, chopped

¼ red onion, thinly sliced

½ cucumber, cut into ½ rounds

Handful of raisins or dried cranberries or both

Handful of walnuts

Wash all greens and dry in a salad spinner.

Finely chop parsley, purslane, lamb's quarters, arugula, dill, basil.

Ribbon-cut kale and place in a small bowl; massage with a dash of olive oil and a pinch of salt until softened and set aside. Ribbon-cut romaine, slice red onion and cucumber, and put all ingredients in a large salad bowl. Add raisins/cranberries and walnuts.

For the Dressing

7 tablespoons extra-virgin olive oil

Juice of 1 orange

1 clove crushed garlic

3 tablespoons apple cider vinegar

2 tablespoons agave or sweetener of choice

½ avocado, mashed

¼ cup basil, finely chopped

Pinch or two of herbes de Provence

Pinch of Himalayan or Celtic salt and pepper

Add dressing slowly to the salad bowl and lightly toss, adding more dressing as needed. This salad likes to be on the wet side.

Whisk all ingredients until well blended. Taste for seasoning and sweetness.

TO SERVE

Mound the salad in the center of a large bowl. Garnish with almonds or walnuts.

Spinach Salad

SERVES 1-2

Need some iron? Vitamin A, E, C, and K? Well, look no longer. Spinach is your veggie.

Spinach is full of antioxidants and lutein for healthy eyes. Some like to lightly steam it and others like to eat it raw. When dining out, I see spinach salads on the menu with bacon, egg, and heavy dressing. This is an easy salad to alter when dining out. Ask the server to leave off the bacon, egg, and dressing, and substitute with avocado and thinly sliced onion. Ask for olive oil and lemon on the side, add a little grind of fresh pepper, and ta-dah, a healthy meal.

There's nothing like the taste of fresh spinach from your garden or the farmers' market. This spinach salad recipe is simple and makes a delicious satisfying meal.

1 bunch of spinach leaves, washed and dried; if leaves are very large, cut in half

¼ red onion, thinly sliced

½ cucumber, cut into thin rounds

8 raw black kalamata olives, pits removed and olives cut in half

2 tablespoons mint leaves, finely chopped

¼ red sweet pepper, very thinly sliced

½ orange or ripe pear, roughly cut

Handful of coarsely chopped walnuts or pecans

For the Dressing

3 tablespoons extra-virgin olive oil

1 teaspoon apple cider vinegar

1 clove garlic, crushed

½ teaspoon mustard

1 orange, juiced

Touch of sweetener if needed

Pinch of Himalayan salt and freshly ground pepper

Whisk until blended and emulsified.

Put spinach into a large bowl and mix with remaining salad ingredients.

Slowly add dressing, stopping to lightly toss. Amount of dressing used is your choice.

TO SERVE
Mound the salad in the center of a large bowl or plate. Sprinkle with nuts.
Drizzle a stream of dressing around the rim of the plate.

Tip { Best served when the salad is very cold. After you wash your spinach, wrap in paper or kitchen towel, place in a plastic bag. Refrigerate while making the dressing. Put salad plates in the freezer for about 15–20 minutes before plating to ensure the salad stays chilled while consuming.

House Salad

From my house to your house with love.

SERVES 2

1 corn kernel, cut from the cob

½ cup cilantro, finely chopped

½ cup celery, finely chopped

½ cup cucumber, chopped small

½ cup tomato, chopped small

½ cup red onion or 2 scallions, chopped small

1 avocado, sliced diagonally in shell and kept together to fan on top of salad

3 romaine lettuce leaves

For the Dressing

3 tablespoons extra-virgin olive oil

⅛ teaspoon Dijon or homemade mustard (See p. 61)

½ lemon or lime, juiced

1 tablespoon agave, or sweetener of choice

Pinch of salt

3 grinds of black pepper

Whisk all ingredients together until smooth and blended.

Lightly toss all the salad ingredients with the dressing except the avocado and lettuce leaves.

TO SERVE

Place lettuce leaves in the bottom of a large flat bowl. Butter lettuce works well for this dish. If using romaine, cut off the hard bottom piece of the stem and use 2–3 leaves.

Place a mound of salad in the middle of the leaves and fan avocado slices on top of each mound. Garnish with chopped chives or scallion and a piece of flat-leaf parsley.

Kale

Kale is king or queen of dark leafy greens and the one vegetable I eat almost every day. It contains vitamin A, K, and beta-carotene. Kale is high in vitamin C and magnesium. It has anti-inflammatory and anticancer properties. It's loaded with antioxidants, which helps age-related diseases and cancer. Kale is low in calories; it controls blood sugar levels and is good for the heart. Kale has a higher absorption of calcium than milk. Kale salads taste great and are very simple to prepare.

I grow kale in my garden and use it in my morning juice. Kale salad holds up well with dressing and even tastes great the next day after it's had time to marinate. When I bring kale salad to a potluck or dinner party, I always leave with an empty bowl. It has a slightly bitter taste, but when oil or dressing is massaged into the leaves, the bitterness disappears and the leaves wilt and relax just like we do after a massage. Kale might become one of your favorite greens.

Flat dinosaur kale has slender stalks. Curly-leaf kale is self-descriptive.

Tip { To destem kale, tear off the leaf from the stem by hand or place leaf on a cutting board and use a sharp knife slicing down close to the stem. To cut into ribbon strips, lay or bunch leaves on top of one another and slice into small ribbon-like strips.

Hail for Kale

SERVES 2–4

2 bunches dino kale (the flat kind), washed and destemmed, and cut into ribbons
¼ head red cabbage, thinly sliced
½ cup fresh corn kernels, cut from the cob

½ tomato, chopped
1 small piece of onion, finely chopped
½ cup parsley, chopped
½ cup pecans, roughly chopped

Place all ingredients except pecans in a large bowl.

Papaya Vinaigrette Dressing

1 papaya, peeled and diced
2 tablespoons apple cider vinegar
Juice of 1 lime
2 tablespoons extra-virgin olive oil

2 tablespoon agave, or sweetener of choice
1 tablespoon mint, chopped
1 clove garlic, chopped

Whisk together all ingredients except the chopped papaya. When blended well, mash ⅓ of the papaya and add to the dressing mix and whisk to blend.

Pour ⅓ of the dressing over the kale salad. Use your hands to massage the dressing into the kale. Add more dressing as needed. Add chopped papaya, cabbage, corn, tomatoes, onion, and parsley and gently toss together. Let rest for 2 hours in the refrigerator to allow kale to soften and the dressing permeate the leaves or eat immediately.

TO SERVE
Pile onto a large simple plate and sprinkle whole or chopped pecans on top.

Upscale Kale Salad
SERVES 2–4

2 bunches of kale, wash and destemmed	1 orange or tangerine, segmented
1 cup raisins or dried cranberries	¾ cup cashews, roughly chopped, or whole pecans
¼ sweet or red onion, thinly sliced	Sliced bell peppers, grated carrot or parsnip, optional

For the Dressing

1 orange, juiced	Pinch of Himalayan salt to taste
6 tablespoons extra-virgin olive oil	Pepper to taste
2 tablespoons apple cider vinegar	A dash of coconut aminos, tamari, Bragg's, or nama shoyu
1 small clove garlic, minced or crushed	
3 tablespoons agave, or 3 dates soaked and blended with a small amount of water	

Place all dressing ingredients in a bowl except olive oil and whisk until blended. Slowly add olive, whisking to emulsify.

Taste for seasonings and adjust if necessary.

Place kale in a bowl and pour ½ of the dressing on top. Massage dressing into the kale with your hands. You will know when it's ready as the leaves begin to soften quite quickly. Add more dressing as needed to soften leaves. Add raisins or cranberries, onion, orange, or tangerine, segmented, and ½ of the chopped cashews. Let the kale mixture rest to marinate in the refrigerator or eat immediately.

TO SERVE
Mound kale salad in the middle of a large plate, sprinkle with balance of chopped cashews and a few orange segments. Serve cold or at room temperature.

Tip { Kale salad holds up well refrigerated in a closed container for a day or two.

Alternate Salad Dressing

6 tablespoons extra-virgin olive oil

½ lemon, juiced

¼ cups apple cider vinegar

1 clove garlic, minced

1 tablespoon agave or sweetener of choice

½ teaspoon Dijon mustard (not raw) or homemade (see recipe on p. 61)

Dash of coconut aminos or tamari

Himalayan salt and pepper to taste

Place all dressing ingredients in a bowl and whisk in the oil until smooth and creamy.

Taste for seasoning, and make adjustments if necessary.

Parsley Salad

SERVES 2

This is so simple, but I had to put it in the book because it is so delicious and healthy and is one of my favorite salads. This recipe says serves 2, but I usually eat the whole thing myself.

2 bunches of Italian flat-leaf parsley, stems removed and leaves finely chopped

¼ sweet red pepper, thinly sliced

1 handful cashews, chopped

For the Dressing

½ lemon, juiced

2–3 tablespoons extra-virgin olive oil

Himalayan sea salt to taste

Freshly milled pepper to taste

Whisk together until well blended.

Adjust the amount of dressing you make for this salad to suit your taste.

Place chopped parsley leaves in a bowl with the red pepper slices and lightly toss.

TO SERVE
Place parsley mixture in a shallow decorative bowl and sprinkle chopped cashews on top.

Tip { Of course you can add other things, but I like it plain best of all.

Granny's Progressive Waldorf Salad

SERVES 2–3

This salad is easy to make, rich and hearty, and a satisfying stand-alone meal.

Original Waldorf salads are saturated with mayonnaise or whipped cream and never appealed to me, so way back in the '70s, I just created my own. Growing up, my children loved the taste of this salad, and it kept them from the alternative by satisfying their taste for sweets.

2 green or crisp, firm apples, coarsely chopped

2 stalks of celery, chopped

Handful of raisins; if they are not plump, soak in filtered water for 15 minutes

½ cup walnuts and pecans, broken or chopped

Generous handful of grapes cut in half, your choice of color

½ lemon, juiced

Mix gently lemon juice with apples to prevent them from darkening

For the Dressing

½ cup almond, soaked for 4 hours (alternative would be 3–4 tablespoons of almond butter)

¼ cup pine nuts

¾ cup water (use at your discretion if using almond butter)

1 clove garlic, crushed

Pinch of Himalayan or Celtic sea salt

1 tablespoon lemon juice

3 medjool dates, pitted, or sweetener of choice

2 tablespoons Irish moss gel (optional)

⅓ cup extra-virgin olive oil

Or use mayonnaise in place of dressing. (See recipe on page 61.)

Place all dressing ingredients except olive oil in a high-powered blender. Blend at medium speed while drizzling in the oil. Blend until creamy and smooth. If you prefer a thicker dressing, just add more pine nuts or some cashews. Chill for 4 hours.

TO SERVE

Slowly pour ⅓ of the dressing on salad and toss well. Use as much of the dressing as suits your taste. Place a lettuce leaf on a salad plate or in a shallow bowl. I like to use butter lettuce as it curves perfectly for holding Waldorf salad. Place a large scoop of the salad into the leaf and garnish with grapes and chopped nuts.

Beet Salad

I've always loved beets especially slow roasted, but now I can't get enough of this raw beet salad. I think it's addicting.

2 beets, peeled and grated (use grater blade attachment of food processor or grate by hand)

For the Dressing

½ cup apple cider vinegar   2-3 tablespoons agave or sweetener of choice to taste

Whisk dressing and taste for seasonings. Use a pinch of salt if necessary. I prefer my dressing just slightly on the sweet side. Pour dressing over beets and let rest for 10–15 minutes. I always drink any dressing left in the bottom of the salad bowl.

Cold Noodle Salad

This makes a perfect lunch with some of your favorite fragrant Asian seasonings, and you will certainly feel better after eating this compared to noodles containing wheat or gluten. If you do not have a spiralizer, use a potato peeler and make noodles by peeling the zucchini into thin strips. They will look like a flat fettuccini noodle. For either method, remove the skin from zucchini, or leave it on, your choice.

Peel zucchini, cut in half, and spiralize. Place into a bowl and sprinkle lightly with salt. Let the zucchini rest for 15 minutes. Break or cut into shorter lengths if preferred.

2 scallions, chopped

1 small carrot, peeled and cut into thin diagonal pieces then into thin matchstick strips

4 tablespoons cilantro, chopped

½ cup Chinese snow peas, stem string removed and chopped

½ cup bean sprouts

2 tablespoon black sesame seeds

Pat zucchini dry and squeeze lightly with a paper towel to remove any excess liquid. Place all ingredients in a bowl, reserving the sesame seeds and ½ of the scallions.

For the Dressing

2 tablespoons sesame seed oil (not raw, but you can make your own by blending sesame seeds and extra-virgin olive oil and letting it rest for two weeks; strain and it is ready to use)

3 tablespoons extra-virgin olive oil

3 tablespoons apple cider vinegar

1 clove garlic, minced

½–1 teaspoon ginger, minced or grated

Dash of coconut aminos or tamari

1 tablespoon agave, or sweetener of your choice

Pinch of Himalayan sea salt

A pinch or so of chili pepper flakes

Place all ingredients except olive oil into a small mixing bowl. Slowly add olive oil, whisking to emulsify. Taste for balance of seasonings and adjust to taste.

Squeeze the liquid from the zucchini and place all the salad ingredients in a bowl. Slowly mix in dressing until noodles are well coated.

TO SERVE
Place in individual shallow serving bowls or large dinner plate. Mound in the center and sprinkle sesame seeds and chopped scallion on top of each portion. If there is any dressing left, serve in a small condiment dish on the side of the plate.

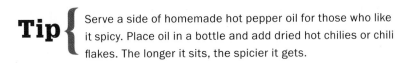

Tip { Serve a side of homemade hot pepper oil for those who like it spicy. Place oil in a bottle and add dried hot chilies or chili flakes. The longer it sits, the spicier it gets.

Ranch, Italian Herb Vinaigrette,and
Secret Sauce Thousand Island
Dressings

Dressings

SECRET SAUCE THOUSAND ISLAND

1 cup cashews, soaked for 4 hours

5–6 halved sun-dried tomatoes, soaked to soften

3 tablespoons lemon juice (about ½ lemon)

1 teaspoon of stone-ground mustard or mustard seeds

Salt to taste

¼ onion, chopped very finely

1 stalk celery, chopped very finely

Blend all ingredients, except onion and celery, adding enough water to get mixture moving. Start with ½ cup, adding more if necessary to make thick and pourable.

When smooth texture has been reached, remove from blender and place into a bowl. Stir in reserved onions and celery just to give the dressing a little chunk.

Let dressing rest in refrigerator overnight in a closed container for best taste.

BASIC VINAIGRETTE

This is a very simple dressing to carry with you in a small bottle when dining out at restaurants. This dressing usually goes well with most salads, and you can be assured that you will have the best extra-virgin olive oil and ingredients.

1 large lemon, juiced

1 clove garlic, minced

Himalayan sea salt to taste

Freshly milled pepper to taste

Pinch of paprika

Pinch of herbes de Provence or other favorite herbs

6 tablespoons extra-virgin olive oil

Place all ingredients except olive oil into a bowl.

Pour olive oil slowly over the basic ingredients, whisking briskly as you pour. Adjust for taste.

ITALIAN HERB VINAIGRETTE

½ cup extra-virgin olive oil

1 tablespoon apple cider vinegar

3 tablespoons lemon juice

2 teaspoons agave or sweetener of choice

Pinch of salt to taste

Freshly milled black pepper to taste

1 teaspoon mixed herbs, oregano, rosemary, thyme

1 teaspoon fresh basil, chopped

Whisk to blend together.

Place all ingredients except olive oil into a bowl.

Pour olive oil slowly over the basic ingredients, whisking briskly as you pour. Adjust for taste.

RANCH DRESSING

MAKES 1 CUP

Good for salads or dips.

1 cup mayonnaise (see recipe on p. 61)

½ teaspoon fresh chives, finely chopped or dried

¼ teaspoon dried tarragon

½ teaspoon fresh parsley, finely chopped, or ⅛ teaspoon dried parsley

¼ teaspoon oregano

½ teaspoon garlic powder

1 teaspoon lemon juice

Fresh milled pepper to taste

Himalayan sea salt to taste

Place all ingredients in a high-powered blender and blend until smooth.

Store in an airtight container in the refrigerator.

Tip { Add ½ avocado and blend to make a thick dip.

Seaweed

Seaweed is an algae. They thrive in mineral-rich environments. They absorb and supply us with calcium, magnesium, potassium, iron, and iodine. Seaweed is especially good for women and is known to help regulate hormones and enrich the metabolism. Both men and women require vitamin A in the form of beta-carotene, vitamins B_1, B_2, B_6, niacin, vitamin C, and E found in seaweed. Also, it has trace amounts of vitamin B_{12}, which usually does not occur in plant-based foods. Seaweed contains traces of omega-6 and omega-3 fatty acids and produce antioxidants. Seaweed is known to cleanse the body of toxins and is good for hair and nail growth. Could seaweed be a secret for a long and healthy life? To me it is, and I regard seaweed as vegan seafood.

If you've ordered a seaweed salad in a Japanese restaurant, many times it is a very bright green. I'm told this kind of seaweed has coloring added, and I've always wondered if it was actually seaweed. The dried sea vegetables I buy come in a variety of colors and textures, including red, white, clear, green, and black, but nothing like the "neon" green. There are many forms of seaweed: palm, nori, dulse, hijiki, arame, kombu, and wakame, to name just a few. Fresh is best and can be purchased at Asian markets. But dried sea vegetables work too if you know the supplier and it's harvested from clean waters.

Seaweed Salad

....

⅓–½ cup dried seaweed

....

Seaweed takes 15 minutes to soak, drain, and use.

For the Dressing

....

2 tablespoons sesame seed oil

1 teaspoon coconut aminos or tamari

½ clove garlic, crushed

Pinch of chili flakes if you like a little spice

1 tablespoon extra-virgin olive oil

⅛ teaspoon fresh ginger, grated

1 tablespoon apple cider vinegar

....

Whisk all ingredients until well incorporated and pour on salad.

Top with sesame seeds and green part of a scallion.

Tomato
Arugula Tapenade

cheese, Pâtés, TAPENADES, WRAPS, and ROLLS

Cheese

Some vegetarians find it difficult to give up cheese even though some know it's not the best food to consume. Cheese is very high in calories and fat. To that, add sodium and cholesterol. Cheese may taste good, but like all animal products, there is no reason to eat it when you have healthy alternatives.

Try some of these cheese recipes, and soon you will be making your own creations. In no time, you will lose the desire to consume dairy cheese. Basic raw cheeses may contain nuts, probiotics, or rejuvelac for curing, lemon, salt, nutritional yeast, and some Irish moss for thickening. You can add a variety of herbs to enhance the flavor.

Basic Herbed Cheese

2 cups macadamia, cashews, pine nuts, or almonds, soaked 4 hours in 3 cups filtered water

1 teaspoons lemon juice

½ teaspoon Himalayan or Celtic sea salt

½ teaspoon probiotic powder

1 tablespoon nutritional yeast (not raw)

1 or more cups of water as needed

Blend all ingredients in a high-powered blender until smooth. Start by adding ½ cup water, blend; add more water as needed using a tamp to scrape sides down and to keep nut mixture moving. Add more water a tablespoon at a time if necessary. Texture should be smooth and very thick. Taste and adjust salt.

Place a strainer over a bowl and line it with cheesecloth. Scrape cheese mixture into a strainer and place another piece of cheesecloth on top. Wrap up the sides of the cloth to cover the mixture and place a weight on top just heavy enough to slowly and gently push out the extra liquid. Leave for 24 hours to culture at room temperature.

Remove cheese from cloth and place in a covered container and store in the refrigerator. Or place in a small mold with removable bottom that has been lined with clear kitchen wrap. Cheese firms up as it chills. Finished cheese can be stored in the refrigerator for at least a week.

If you choose, shape cheese in a mold and dehydrate for 10 hours at 105 degrees to give the cheese a rind. Remove from dehydrator and place the cheese in the refrigerator until it sets before removing mold.

Tip { After cheese has cured, you can mix in 1 teaspoon coconut aminos, tamari, miso, nama shoyu, or Bragg's; herbs of choice, including chives, garlic, black pepper, dill, and sun-dried tomato. or form into a wedge, log, or ball and coat with fresh herbs. Serve with flax crackers, veggies, or use on raw bread or pizzas, roll in nori sushi, collard wraps, and much more.

Cream Cheese

2 cups cashews, soaked 4 hours in 3 cups filtered water

1 teaspoon lemon juice

½ teaspoon Himalayan or Celtic sea salt

4 tablespoons Irish moss paste

½ teaspoon probiotic powder

1 tablespoon nutritional yeast, not raw

1 cup water, or more if needed

Blend all ingredients in a high-powered blender until smooth. Start with 1 cup of water, adding more if needed to make a smooth but thick mixture. Taste to see if all the nuts are broken down and the mixture is smooth, creamy, and thick.

Place a strainer lined with cheesecloth over a bowl. Scrape cheese mixture into a strainer and place another piece of cheesecloth on top. Wrap up the sides of the cloth to cover the mixture and place a weight on top just heavy enough to slowly and gently push out the extra liquid. Leave for 24 hours to culture at room temperature.

Remove cheese from cloth and place in a covered container and store in the refrigerator. Cheese firms up as it chills. Can be stored in the refrigerator for at least a week.

To make creamy dill cheese, add 2 tablespoons finely chopped dill after the cheese is removed from the cheesecloth. Mix well until incorporated.

Cheddar Cheese

2 cups macadamia nuts, soaked 4 hours in 3 cups filtered water

1 tablespoon paprika

1 teaspoon lemon juice

½ teaspoon Himalayan or Celtic sea salt

½ teaspoon probiotic powder

1 tablespoon nutritional yeast (not raw)

⅛ teaspoon turmeric

⅛ teaspoon paprika

1 cup water, or more if needed

Blend all ingredients in a high-powered blender until smooth. Start with 1 cup of water and add more if needed to make a smooth but thick mixture. Taste to see if all the nuts are broken down and the mixture is creamy and thick.

Place a strainer over a bowl and line it with cheesecloth. Scrape cheese mixture into a strainer and place another piece of cheesecloth on top. Wrap up the sides of the cloth to cover the mixture and place a weight on top just heavy enough to slowly and gently push out the extra liquid. Leave for 24 hours to culture at room temperature.

Remove cheese from cloth and place in a covered container and store in the refrigerator. Cheese firms up as it chills. Finished cheese can be stored in the refrigerator for at least a week.

Line a mold the size you want your cheese to be with clear wrap and place the cheese in the mold, pressing it in. Tap on the counter to remove any air. Refrigerate until it hardens.

Pimento Cheese

½ cup red bell pepper, finely chopped
2 cups cashews, soaked 1 hour in 3 cups
  filtered water
2 teaspoons lemon juice
⅛ teaspoon paprika

½ teaspoon Himalayan or Celtic sea salt
½ teaspoon probiotic powder
1 tablespoon nutritional yeast (not raw)
1 cup water or more if needed

Put chopped red bell peppers in a small glass container. Sprinkle salt over the top and cover with oil. Dehydrate at 110 degrees for 1–2 hours until they soften.

Drain peppers from the oil. Blend all ingredients except peppers in a high-powered blender until smooth. Start with 1 cup of water and add more if needed to make a smooth thick mixture without lumps. Keep the mixture as thick as possible. Add 1 tablespoon of the red peppers and blend until incorporated.

Place a strainer lined with cheesecloth over a bowl. Scrape cheese mixture into a strainer and place another piece of cheesecloth on top. Wrap up the sides of the cloth to cover the mixture and place a weight on top just heavy enough to slowly and gently push out the extra liquid. Leave for 24 hours to culture at room temperature.

Remove cheese from cloth and, with a spatula, blend in the remaining red peppers. Taste for salt. Place in a covered container and store in the refrigerator. Cheese firms up as it chills. Finished cheese can be stored in the refrigerator for at least a week.

Shape by hand, or use a mold to shape as desired. Line a mold with clear wrap and pack the cheese firmly into the mold, tapping container on the counter to remove any air. Refrigerate until it hardens and lift out the clear wrap.

Sour Cream

1 cup cashews, soaked for 4 hours

½ teaspoon probiotics, for curing

1 teaspoon unpasteurized light miso paste

¼ teaspoon salt

3 tablespoons lemon juice

¾–1 cup water

Place all ingredients into a high-powered blender and blend until smooth and creamy, adding more water if necessary. Place in a covered container and store in the refrigerator. Mixture thickens as it chills. For thinner consistency, add water as needed. For thicker consistency, add 2 tablespoons of Irish moss paste. Mixture can be put in a squeeze bottle for topping and decorating.

Tip { Cut recipe in half if you only need a small amount for topping a dish.

Cashew Parmesan

1 cup cashews
1 clove garlic

⅛ teaspoon Himalayan salt or to taste

Pulse-chop all ingredients in a food processor until it looks like the texture of Parmesan cheese. You want the pieces very tiny. Add more salt if needed to taste.

Will keep in refrigerator for a several weeks. Use on pastas, salads, main dishes, and vegetables.

Pâtés, Hummus, and Tapenades

Pâtés are a great staple to keep in your refrigerator for moments you might need a quick snack. Pâtés are very versatile and, because they are satisfying, can help you stay on the raw path. When you don't have time to fix a meal, all you need is a hummus or pâté, a lettuce or collard leaf, a nori sheet, or a few matchstick veggies, and you have an enjoyable snack.

Zucchini Hummus

2 zucchinis, peeled and coarsely chopped
1 lemon, juiced
3 cloves garlic, minced
1 cup raw tahini
¼ cup sesame seeds
½ teaspoon Himalayan sea salt or to taste

Freshly milled pepper to taste
½ teaspoon cumin
Water as needed
3 tablespoons extra-virgin olive oil
Paprika

Place all ingredients except for the olive oil and paprika in blender. Blend, adding water a little at a time to make a thick, smooth consistency. Taste for seasonings. A little bit more tahini, more salt, or jalapeño? You decide.

Place on a flat plate and create a shallow well in the center of the hummus with a tablespoon. Add the olive oil to the well, sprinkle with paprika, and garnish with finely chopped parsley.

Cashew Hummus

1 cup cashews, soaked for 4 hours

1 tablespoon lemon juice

3 tablespoons tahini

1–2 cloves garlic

½ teaspoon cumin

Himalayan or Celtic sea salt to taste

Water as needed to make mixture smooth

Place all ingredients in a high-powered blender, adding water to keep the mixture moving and on the thick side. Blend until smooth.

Serve with flax crackers, roll into a wrap, or use as a dip with raw veggies.

Cashew Hummus

Tzaziki

In Greece, this dish is called *tzaziki*. In India, it's called *raita*, but whatever it's called, it tastes great.

1 cup cashews, soaked for 4 hours	1 cucumber, seeded and finely chopped
½ cup pine nuts, soaked for 4 hours	1 scallion, chopped
1 tablespoon lemon juice	Himalayan salt to taste
1 teaspoon of extra-virgin olive oil	1 tablespoon fresh dill, chopped
½ cup water	

Lightly salt cucumbers and let rest for 30 minutes to release liquid. Blend cashews, pine nuts, lemon juice, and olive oil in high-powered blender, adding water a little at a time to maintain a creamy consistency. When texture is smooth, scrape into food processor. Add remaining ingredients except dill and pulse-chop 4 times.

Place mixture in a container and incorporate chopped dill. Chill in refrigerator 4 hours or overnight. If mixture is too thick after it chills, add a tablespoon or two of filtered water to thin. Texture should be creamy and smooth. More chopped cucumber may be added if desired.

(For sprouting garbanzo beans for hummus, see sprouting instructions, page 115)

Mushroom Pâté

2 large portobello mushroom caps, or 12–15 baby portobello mushrooms	2 tablespoons extra-virgin olive oil
½ cup walnuts	2 tablespoons tamari, nama shoyu, or Bragg's
1 clove garlic	Freshly milled black pepper

Wipe mushrooms' caps with a damp paper towel. Remove stem and cut off a small piece of the bottom. Slice mushrooms and marinate in oil and coconut aminos or tamari, including stems. Marinate for 30 minutes, turning occasionally.

Place walnuts in food processor and pulse until broken down. Add garlic and marinated mushrooms. Pulse-chop until mixture is incorporated and slightly chunky. Taste for seasonings and adjust to taste.

Serve with flax crackers or roll with other vegetables into a wrap.

Pumpkin and Sunflower Seed Pâté

1 cup pumpkin seeds

1 cup sunflower seeds

2 tablespoons lemon juice

½ cup scallions

2 tablespoons tahini

1 tablespoon coconut aminos, miso paste, tamari, nama shoyu, or Bragg's

1-2 small clove garlic, crushed

Himalayan sea salt to taste

Water, start with ½ cup and add more if needed

Grind pumpkin seeds and sunflower seeds in a high-powered blender, spice or coffee grinder. Place seed mixture and remaining ingredients in food processor and pulse-chop until smooth, adding water as needed.

Serve with flax crackers or roll in a wrap.

Red Pepper Pâté

1 cup walnuts

½ cup cashews

1 red pepper, seeded and cut in chunks

1 celery rib, cut in pieces

1 scallion, cut in pieces

3 tablespoons coconut aminos or tamari

3-4 grinds Himalayan or Celtic sea salt

1 tablespoon extra-virgin olive oil

⅛ teaspoon curry powder

1 clove garlic

In a food processor, place walnuts and cashews. Pulse-chop 4–5 times to break down. Add remaining ingredients and pulse until smooth.

Use as a dip for vegetables or crackers, wrapped in a nori sheet or lettuce leaves with raisins and sprouts.

Tapenades for Breads or Crackers

1. **Tomato Arugula Tapenade**: Brush a piece of Mediterranean flatbread (see page 99) with crushed garlic–infused extra-virgin olive oil. Make a mixture of chopped tomatoes, ribbon-sliced arugula and basil, very thin slices of zucchini, and red or sweet onion. Sprinkle with a dash of olive oil, a pinch of salt and pepper, and spoon on to the top of the flatbread.

2. **Olive Tapenade**: 1 cup raw chopped olives; ¼ cup softened sun-dried tomatoes, chopped; 1 tablespoon capers; 1 crushed garlic clove; 1 tablespoon chopped basil; pinch each of thyme, oregano, rosemary, and marjoram; salt and pepper to taste. Mix well and spoon on top of flatbread.

3. **Mushroom Tapenade**: In your food processor, place ½ cup walnuts, 1 cup portobello mushrooms, ¼ piece of a small onion, 1 tablespoons of coconut aminos or tamari, and pulse-chop until incorporated. Add a few grinds of fresh ground pepper, taste for saltiness, and top the flatbread with mixture, adding a ribbon of basil garnish.

Wrap, Roll, and Assembly

Wraps and rolls are staples in a raw food home. They are simple and quick to make, and the pâté and hummus fillings can be stored in the refrigerator for a few days. The wrap, or outside of the filling, consists of collard leaves with stems removed, romaine or butter lettuce leaves, cabbage leaves, untoasted raw nori sheets, and a variety of corn, spinach, and coconut tortillas.

The fillings for the wraps and rolls are endless combinations of pâtés, avocado, raw cheeses, hummus, vegetables, fruits, and herbs.

Lettuce Wrap Salad

SERVES 2–3

I love these because they are so satisfying and quick to make.

- 1½ cup jicama, finely chopped
- 1½ cup shiitake mushrooms, finely chopped
- ¼ cup red onion, finely chopped
- ¾ cup red bell pepper, finely chopped
- 1 cup bean sprouts, finely chopped
- 2 scallions, finely chopped

- ½ cup Chinese pea pods, finely sliced
- 3 tablespoons tamari
- 1 tablespoon lime juice
- 1 tablespoon extra-virgin olive oil
- 1 head butter lettuce leaves
- ½ cup mint leaves
- ½ bunch cilantro, with stems

Wash lettuce leaves and wrap in paper or kitchen towels. Place in refrigerator to chill and crisp.

Marinate chopped vegetables except lettuce, mint, and cilantro, in oil and tamari for 10 minutes.

TO SERVE

Place filling on plate and serve lettuce leaves, cilantro, and mint on a separate plate.

Make wrap by placing filling on a butter lettuce leaf, along with a piece of mint, cilantro leaves, and a drizzle each of the peanut, cilantro, and tamari sauces.

Filling can be served warm or cold. I like it warm especially with crisp chilled lettuce leaves.

Tip Place ingredients in dehydrator at 110 degrees for 1 hour to warm and slightly soften vegetables.

Sauces

MAKE 3 DIPPING SAUCES, WHICH CAN BE USED FOR ANY WRAP

PEANUT SAUCE

- ¼ cup raw peanut butter or raw almond butter
- 1 garlic clove, minced or crushed
- Juice of 1 lime
- 2 tablespoons agave nectar
- 3 tablespoons tamari or nama shoyu

- 3 tablespoons water or as needed to desired texture
- 2 teaspoons grated ginger or pinch of powdered ginger
- Pinch crushed red pepper flakes to taste; or for a spicier version, add finely chopped serrano chili.

In a mixing bowl, whisk together nut butter, garlic, limejuice, agave nectar, tamari, water, ginger, red pepper flakes. Mix until smooth, adding water as needed to reach pourable consistency.

CILANTRO SAUCE

½ cup cilantro, finely chopped

Juice from ½ lime

1 tablespoon of water

Dash of sweetener of choice

Stir until smooth.

COCONUT AMINOS OR TAMARI

2 tablespoons coconut aminos or tamari

2 tablespoon water

Stir together.

Filling Ingredients for Wraps and Rolls

PÂTÉS AND HUMMUS
Red pepper pâté, zucchini hummus, garbanzo bean hummus, basil garlic hummus, olive tapenade, or hummus.

VEGETABLE FILLINGS
Matchstick or julienne vegetables, including the following: carrots, cucumbers, jicama, sweet bell peppers, zucchini, mushrooms, and spinach.

SAVORY FILLINGS
Pâtés, hummus, sprouts, lettuce, spinach, avocado, coconut meat, sun-dried tomato, black olives, capers, and nut cheese.

SWEET FILLINGS
Raw almond or cashew butter, bananas, mango, papaya, pear, strawberries, blueberries, raspberries, blackberries, peaches, plums, kiwi, cherries, dried coconut, apricots, figs, cacao truffles, chopped nuts, sweet cream cheese, ice cream, raisins, and dates.

SAUCES FOR WRAPS AND ROLLS TO DRIBBLE ON OR DIP INTO
Cacao sauce, raspberry sauce, apricot sauce, tahini, lemon dressing, tamari dipping sauce, raw peanut butter dipping sauce, lime dipping sauce, cashew cream sauce.

TORTILLAS AND CREPE SHELLS

Savory or sweet, tortilla wraps are a treat for a raw food diet. Bring out your inner chef and be creative. Fill shells with a raw version of old favorite flavors, or create some new ones. Tortillas can range in color depending on ingredients. Enjoy a lively dark green by using spinach, a rich roasted yellow using corn or sweet yellow bell pepper, and red or orange by using sweet potato, butternut squash, or beet. A variety of colors for a large social gathering is always a big hit.

Corn Tortillas

6–8 ears corn, kernels cut off the cob

½ cup ground golden flaxseeds (ground in a spice or coffee grinder)

¼ cup diced yellow onion

⅛ teaspoon Himalayan or Celtic sea salt

¼ teaspoon combined Mexican seasonings, cumin, oregano, and garlic powder

1 teaspoon extra-virgin olive oil

Water if necessary

Blend all ingredients except flax meal in a high-powered blender until smooth, adding water if needed to make a smooth texture. Add flax meal and adjust liquid if necessary. Blend into a smooth, thick, but pourable consistency. Taste and adjust for seasonings. Pour 2–3 tablespoons on a nonstick dehydrator sheet and shape into rounds with spatula or back of a tablespoon. Dehydrate for 5 hours at 110 degrees. When dry on top, flip onto dehydrator mesh screen and dehydrate another 5–6 hours or until tortilla is dry yet still pliable. *Be careful not to overdehydrate.* Store in a ziplock bag in refrigerator. Will last three days.

Sweet Red Pepper Coconut Wrap

7 Thai baby coconuts, meat only

2 red bell peppers

2 dates, soaked

¼ cup pine nuts

Himalayan or Celtic sea salt

Water as needed

Blend all ingredients except flax meal in a high-powered blender until smooth, adding water or apple juice as needed to make a smooth texture. Add flax meal and adjust liquid if necessary. Blend into a smooth, thick, but pourable consistency. Taste and adjust for seasonings. Pour 2–3 tablespoons on a nonstick dehydrator sheet and shape into rounds with a spatula or back of a tablespoon. Dehydrate for 5 hours at 110 degrees. When dry on top, flip onto dehydrator mesh screen and dehydrate another 5–6 hours or until dry yet still pliable. *Be careful not to overdehydrate.* Store in a ziplock bag in refrigerator. Will last three days.

Tip { Recipes call for spreading onto nonstick dehydrator sheets into rounds; however, you can spread into one large square and cut into four equal parts.

Verde Tortilla Wrap

1 cup spinach

2 zucchinis, coarsely chopped

½ green bell pepper

¼ medium onion, coarsely chopped

1 avocado, cut into chunks

1 tablespoon parsley

¼ cup basil

1 teaspoon extra-virgin olive oil

½ cup flaxseed, ground into a meal in spice or coffee grinder

Pinch of Himalayan or Celtic sea salt

Water as needed

Blend all ingredients except flax meal in a high-powered blender until smooth, adding water or apple juice as needed to make a smooth texture. Add flax meal and adjust water. Blend into a smooth, thick, but pourable consistency. Taste and adjust for seasonings. Pour 2–3 tablespoons on a nonstick dehydrator sheet and shape into rounds with a spatula or back of a tablespoon. Dehydrate for 5 hours at 110 degrees. When dry on top, flip onto dehydrator mesh screen and dehydrate another 5–6 hours or until dry yet still pliable. *Be careful not to overdehydrate.* Store in a ziplock bag in refrigerator. Will last three days.

Sweet Potato Wrap

2 cups sweet potatoes, peeled and coarsely chopped

3 dates, soaked and pureed, or 1 tablespoon agave or sweetener of choice

½ banana

1 tablespoon extra-virgin olive oil

½ teaspoon cinnamon

Pinch of powdered ginger

¾ cup flaxseed, ground to a meal in spice or coffee grinder

Filtered water or fresh apple juice as needed

Blend all ingredients except flax meal in a high-powered blender until smooth, adding water or apple juice as needed to make a smooth texture. Add flax meal and adjust liquid if necessary. Blend into a smooth, thick, but pourable consistency. Taste and adjust for seasonings. Pour 2–3 tablespoons on a nonstick dehydrator sheet and shape into rounds with a spatula or back of a tablespoon. Dehydrate for 5 hours at 110 degrees. When dry on top, flip onto dehydrator mesh screen and dehydrate another 5–6 hours or until dry yet still pliable. *Be careful not to overdehydrate.* Store in a ziplock bag in refrigerator. Will last three days.

How to assemble a collard wrap

Use large collard leaves with center stem removed. Lay leaf flat on a chopping board and use a sharp knife to slice the stem out. Wash and pat leaves dry. Rub collard leaves with ½ teaspoon lemon juice, ½ teaspoon extra-virgin olive oil, and a pinch of sea salt. Place the shiny side down on a chopping board.

Make a filling of nut mixture containing 1 cup soaked walnuts, small piece of onion, crushed garlic, lemon juice, and salt and pepper to taste. Chop till fine in food processor, or use a tablespoon of pâté or hummus placed about ¾ of the way down toward the end of the collard leaf.

On top of nut mixture or pâté, add an assortment of thinly sliced red or green cabbage, microgreens, matchstick julienne carrots, red bell pepper, scallion, a piece of nori sheet, or coconut meat. Both ends will be open when rolled, so extend a few pieces of vegetables out one side.

Fold the short end over the filling and begin rolling up tightly until you reach the end. Lay roll seam-side down on a plate. Another method to rolling is to overlap two leaves side by side, allowing enough leaf so the sides can be folded in when rolling and the filling becomes closed in a little package.

How to assemble a nori sheet wrap

Use a full sheet of nori, shiny-side down, on a bamboo-rolling mat. A mat helps roll to be tight and even when finished. A rolling mat can be purchased at Asian markets or online. To avoid a soggy roll, make a bed for your filling by placing a dry romaine lettuce leaf or a pile of dry baby spring mix greens at the end closest to you. Continue by placing one layer at a time of your pâté, hummus, and thinly sliced vegetables on top of the lettuce. Keep in mind the ends will be open when finished. You can use some of the vegetables to protrude out both sides so when the roll is cut and stood on end, it will make an attractive serving.

Pile on more filling than you think you need; as you roll tightly, the ingredients will become compressed. When all ingredients are in place, lift the end of the bamboo mat nearest you and fold it over the ingredients. This is where you need to tuck in the vegetables and make that first roll tight.

Continue to carefully roll the nori sheet inside the bamboo roller, applying a light, even pressure. When finished, use even pressure with the bamboo mat so it is tightly rolled. When finished rolling, wet your finger in filtered water and run it over the open edge of the nori sheet. It only needs a small amount to seal. Press with roller to seal. Cut desired-size pieces with a very sharp knife. The nori can be cut in slices or in half diagonally. The longer the filled nori roll rests, the more moisture the sheets absorb, making it rubbery and difficult to chew. Best eaten shortly after making.

Sushi Rice

MAKES 1 CUP

2 cups parsnips, peeled and coarsely chopped

4 tablespoons pine nuts

1 tablespoon coconut aminos or unprocessed white miso paste blended with water to make thin and smooth

Pulse parsnips and pine nuts in food processor into rice-like pieces.

Place parsnip mixture in a mixing bowl and blend in coconut amino or miso paste.

Taste for saltiness and add more if needed.

Tip { Use in nori sheets to make sushi rolls.

ADDITIONAL NORI ROLL FILLINGS

Red pepper pâté, vegetable patties, avocado, umeboshi paste, wasabi, Napa cabbage, romaine leaf, bok choy, sunflower or pea sprouts, dried coconut, cilantro, and mint leaves.

How to assemble a cabbage leaf wrap

There is a trick to getting a whole leaf off a cabbage head. It's done by cutting out the core and placing the cabbage head core-side down into a large bowl of water filled with 2–3 cups of ice. Leave the head in the water for several hours or overnight in the refrigerator, or if left on a kitchen countertop, add more ice cubes. The cabbage leaves will start to open up and you can carefully peel them off whole.

Another way is to cut the cabbage head in half, remove core, and carefully peel off leaves under cold running water. The first method allows larger leaves for rolling.

When assembling a cabbage wrap, trim a small thin strip from the hard-stem end of each leaf to make rolling easier. Leaves may be filled and rolled, or just filled and folded in half, taco style.

How to assemble a lettuce leaf wrap

Use romaine, butter, Belgian endive, or radicchio leaf. Fill leaf with desired ingredients and roll or eat open face. Butter lettuce folds over nicely as it is a soft lettuce.

Belgian endive, also known as French endive, is a thin cylinder of tight pale green leaves. Radicchio is tightly leafed, round, dark red with marbled creamy white streaks running through the leaves. Of the chicory family, it has a tiny bitter taste and might not be everyone's cup of tea. If you like arugula, you might like radicchio.

Quick Lettuce Wrap

Use ½ red cabbage leaf as an individual container cup for each of the following: shredded carrot, thinly sliced cucumber, bean sprouts, and shredded zucchini. Use ½ avocado for each person. Cut avocado in half and remove pit. Slice each half diagonally into strips and remove the meat from the skin with a large tablespoon. Fan the avocado on a plate with the individual filled cabbage leaves surrounding it.

Serve leaves of chilled romaine or butter lettuce on a separate plate with stems of cilantro and mint. Each guest can make his or her own lettuce wrap by placing the filling on the leaf, adding a piece of mint and cilantro, and drizzling it with sauce of choice.

French Endive

Not much work to fill these leaves with a raw hummus, nut butter or vegetables of your liking. French endive leaves are crunchy, and slightly bitter. They make beautiful hors d'oeuvres and a lovely dish for a potluck.

How to assemble a cucumber wrap

Lengthwise, slice an unpeeled English cucumber with mandolin slicer into thin pliable strips. Spread a thin layer of pâté, hummus, or mashed avocado to cover the strip. Cut matchstick vegetables 1 inch longer than the width of the cucumber. Leave an inch's space and start from one end, laying matchstick vegetables in a row evenly across the bottom. Vegetables will protrude from one side. Bring end up to fold over the vegetables. Continue rolling tightly. Use a toothpick to hold together and stand open end on a plate or lay roll seam-end down.

Mashed Parsnips and Cauliflower

CHAPTER 10

vegetables

AND

SIDE DISHES

Modern Brussels Sprouts

SERVES 2

Many people do not care for cooked brussels sprouts, but I think this raw version might change a mind or two. Cruciferous vegetables have wonderful cancer-fighting properties.

½ pound brussels sprouts, very thinly sliced

For the Dressing

2 tablespoons extra-virgin olive oil (or pumpkin seed oil)

1½ tablespoons lemon juice

3 tablespoons green onions or chives, chopped

Himalayan salt and freshly milled pepper to taste

⅓ cup almonds, sliced

In a small mixing bowl, place all dressing ingredients except the almonds.

Whisk until well blended. Taste for seasonings and adjust to taste. Pour dressing over brussels sprouts and toss lightly to coat with the dressing.

TO SERVE

Place on individual salad plate and sprinkle almonds on top, or use a larger bowl for a buffet-style serving or potluck.

Mashed Parsnips and Cauliflower

A delicious replacement for mashed potatoes.

½ cups cashews, soaked 3–4 hours

1½ cups parsnip, peeled and cut into 2–3 in pieces.

½ cup cauliflower, cut into pieces

Juice of ½ lemon

Himalayan sea salt

1 tablespoon extra-virgin olive oil

1 small clove of garlic or scant amount of garlic powder

2 tablespoons of nutritional yeast (not raw)

½ cup filtered water

1 teaspoon truffle oil or pinch of truffle salt (optional)

Freshly milled pepper

Place all ingredients except truffle oil in the food processor and chop fine. Add water to make it a smooth, thick mixture.

If mixture is not smooth enough, transfer to a high-powered blender and blend until smooth. Add a little water at a time if necessary to keep blender spinning. You want the mixture the consistency of mashed potatoes.

Tip { Add truffle oil or salt, or other herbs, to taste.

Ratatouille

SERVES 4–6

Ratatouille originated in the south of France and is a combination of simple stewed vegetables. Traditionally served as a side dish or in crepes and omelets, ratatouille can stand alone as a full meal. There are hundreds of versions of this classic dish, and I'm adding a raw one to the list.

3 tablespoons extra-virgin olive oil

1 medium onion, chopped

1 eggplant, peeled and cut into cubes.

1–2 zucchini, coarsely chopped

2 sweet bell peppers, one red and one yellow, coarsely shopped

4 tomatoes, seeded and coarsely chopped

⅛ teaspoon oregano

⅛ teaspoon marjoram

½ cup raw olives, cut in half

¼ cup capers

Himalayan or Celtic sea salt to taste

Freshly milled pepper

Place eggplant cubes in a colander and sprinkle with salt. Let rest for 1 hour to sweat and release liquid.

Heat olive oil in a glass baking dish in dehydrator at 115 degrees or in a double boiler until warm.

Pat eggplants dry and place all chopped vegetables in baking dish with heated olive oil. Mix to coat. Sprinkle with herbs, salt, and pepper, and mix again. Add 2 tablespoons of water and cover with foil. Dehydrate 6 hours or until vegetables are soft. Adjust seasonings to your liking.

Serve warm or at room temperature.

Good over warm sprouted wild rice (see recipe on page 170).

Stuffed Zucchini Squash Blossoms

SERVES 4–6

This is a summer dish when zucchinis are in peak season.

6–12 zucchinis blossoms with or without mini zucchinis attached

2 tablespoons chives, chopped

1 tablespoon basil, chopped

⅛ teaspoon oregano, ground

1 recipe basic cheese (see recipe on p. 143)

1 tablespoon extra-virgin olive oil

Himalayan salt

Freshly milled pepper

1 large zucchini, thinly sliced, for lining steamer

⅛ teaspoon each, oregano and marjoram, ground

Blend chives, basil, oregano, and marjoram into cheese with a spatula. Add Himalayan salt and freshly milled pepper to taste. Gently open flower and stuff with cheese mixture.

Line a vegetable steamer (bamboo works best) lengthwise with very thin slices of zucchini or lettuce leaves. Place blossoms on top of zucchini or lettuce and lightly sprinkle on olive oil. Cover with foil. Place a glass baking dish with water in dehydrator bottom and set the steamer of blossoms on top. Dehydrate 1–2 hour until wilted and warm.

TO SERVE
Place in a bowl and for an extra treat, drizzle a couple of drops of truffle oil or truffle salt on top.

Jicama Fries

1 jicama

1 tablespoon extra-virgin olive oil

½ teaspoon Himalayan sea salt or to taste

1 tablespoon paprika

½ teaspoon garlic powder

Pinch chili powder if you like it spicy

Peel and slice jicama with a mandolin slicer into even french fry strips, or use a sharp knife. Place in a bowl and add all ingredients, mixing well to coat. Eat as is, or dehydrate for 1 hour at 110 to make them warm. Serve with ketchup (see recipe on page 61).

Kale Chips

Once you make this basic kale chip recipe, you will be inspired to add other herbs and spices, including pizza herbs, Italian mix, herbes de Provence, Mexican spices, cashew cream, and any flavor you crave.

2 bunches kale, either dinosaur or curly

2 tablespoons extra-virgin olive oil

3 tablespoons coconut aminos, tamari, nama shoyu, or Bragg's

Sprinkle of garlic powder

½ cup or more nutritional yeast flakes (not raw)

Remove kale center stem by placing on a chopping board and using a sharp knife. Run tip of knife close to the stem to remove. Cut each leaf in half or leave whole. You want the kale pieces large as they shrink quite a bit in dehydration.

Place kale in a big bowl and add all ingredients except nutritional yeast. Mix well and massage with your hands. Sprinkle on nutritional yeast and mix with thongs, making sure all leaves are coated with yeast. (It gets sticky, so add more nutritional yeast if desired.) Nutritional yeast gives chips a cheesy flavor.

Place strips directly on mesh dehydrator trays for 4–5 hours at 115 degrees. When finished, they should be crispy. It's easy to eat them right off the dehydrator tray before they are finished . . . very addictive!

Nachos This Side of the Border

1 recipe corn chips, made a little thicker to hold the cheese sauce. (See recipe, p. 101.)

CHEESE SAUCE

MAKES 2 CUPS

2 cups cashews, soaked for 4 hours

1 red bell pepper, seeded and cut in half

3 tablespoons nutritional yeast

⅛ teaspoon turmeric

⅛ teaspoon paprika

1 clove garlic, cut in half

⅛ teaspoon salt, or 1 tablespoon coconut aminos, tamari, or nama shoyu

1 cup or more water as needed

Drain and rinse cashews. Place all ingredients in your high-powered blender. Add ½ of the water and blend. Add more water as needed to make a pourable, smooth cheese. Taste for seasonings especially salt, and add more if needed.

Heat cheese in glass container in dehydrator set at 105–110 degrees.

NACHO TOPPINGS

Avocado, chopped

Scallions, chopped

TO ASSEMBLE

Pile corn chips onto a plate. Pour warm cheese sauce over the chips. Add chopped avocado, chopped scallions, chopped tomatoes, and hot peppers if you like.

Mini Tostadas

6–8 ears corn, kernels cut off the cob

½ cup ground golden flax (ground in a spice or coffee grinder)

¼ cup of diced yellow onion

⅛ teaspoon salt

¼ teaspoon combined Mexican seasonings, cumin, oregano, and garlic powder

Mix corn, onion, and salt in the food processor until on the smooth side. Add ground flax and pulse to blend. Sometimes I give the mixture a whirl in my blender to make it smooth.

Drop a tablespoonful at a time onto nonstick dehydrator sheet and smooth into 3" rounds.

Dehydrate for about 8 hours at 110 degrees. Flip directly onto mesh dehydrator screen and dehydrate another 7–8 hours until crispy.

Toppings for the tostadas:

GUACAMOLE

2 avocado, mashed

2 tablespoons onion, chopped finely

1 tomato, chopped finely

2 tablespoons lemon juice

Mix altogether and season to taste with salt, pepper, Mexican seasonings, and if you like it hot, a small piece of jalapeño.

SALSA

1 large or 2 medium tomatoes

3 tablespoons cilantro

2–3 tablespoons onion

1 tablespoon limejuice

Dash of oregano and cumin

Dash of salt and pepper

Pulse in food processor, or chop all by hand.

SOUR CREAM (see recipe on page 146)

TO SERVE:

Stack the tostada chips

A bowl of guacamole

A bowl of salsa

Sour cream in a squeeze bottle

A bowl of chopped scallions.

It's best to have your guests assemble their own when ready to eat as the tostada may soften from the moisture of the toppings if made too far in advance.

Wild, Wild Rice

Rice is a staple in many countries. Served along with meals, it can be simple or full of spices. This Wild Rice version has the flavors from south of the border but with a crunchier texture.

Sprouted wild rice doesn't exactly get those little tails we call sprouts, nor do all the rice kernels open and soften, but enough open if the rice is live and not processed. Sprouting wild rice takes about three days, but you can speed up the process by putting rice in a covered jar or glass bowl and placing on bottom shelf of dehydrator at 110 degrees for 12 hours.

If you choose to sprout on the counter, see sprouting instructions page 115.

1 cup wild rice, sprouted

2 tablespoons extra-virgin olive oil

⅛ teaspoon cumin

2 tablespoons onion, chopped

1 clove garlic, finely minced or crushed

1 cup Roma tomatoes, seeded and chopped

½ cucumber, seeded and chopped

1 scallion, chopped including green part

¼ cup cilantro, chopped

½ cup flat parsley leaves, chopped

2 tablespoons lemon juice

Himalayan sea salt to taste

Toss gently to incorporate.

Mix all ingredients except rice in a large bowl.

Add the rice and mix again.

This can be eaten as a side dish or as a meal in itself.

Tabbouleh

I usually make a large amount to eat for a couple of days. Good served cold or at room temperature.

½ cup sprouted wild rice (see sprouting directions, p. 115) or ½ cup cauliflower

2 medium tomatoes, chopped

1 cucumber, seeded and chopped

1½ cups parsley, finely chopped

2 scallions (green onions), chopped

2 tablespoons fresh mint, chopped

If using cauliflower, pulse-chop in food processor, making into small, rice-size pieces. Place all ingredients into a large salad bowl.

For the Dressing

½ cup extra-virgin olive oil

Juice from 1 lemon, about 3 tablespoons

Himalayan salt and fresh ground pepper to taste

Mix chopped ingredients with dressing and toss well.

Curly Cucumber

SERVES 1–2

1 large English cucumber; if organic, leave skin on

⅓ cup apple cider vinegar

1 tablespoon agave or sweetener of choice

1 scallion, chopped

1 tablespoon hemp seeds

Himalayan sea salt to taste

Cut English cucumber in 3 pieces. Spiralize with straight cutting blade. Cut strips to desired length.

Mix apple cider vinegar with agave or sweetener of choice.

Pour dressing over cucumbers and gently toss.

Add salt to taste. Taste for sweetness.

TO SERVE

Divide into 2 bowls and sprinkle with scallions and hemp seeds. Serve with chopsticks.

Pasta alla checca

main
COURSES

· · · · · · · · · · · · · · · · · · · ·

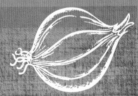

Chili

MAKES APPROXIMATELY 2 QUARTS

For the Base

- 1 cup sun-dried tomatoes, soak until soft about 30 minutes to 1 hour
- 2 cups tomatoes, chopped
- ½ cup carrots, chopped
- 1 small piece jalapeño pepper, minced
- 1 clove garlic

- 2 tablespoons coconut aminos, tamari, nama shoyu, or Bragg's
- 1 tablespoon each extra-virgin olive oil, apple cider vinegar, agave, and chili powder
- 1 teaspoon each cumin, oregano, and paprika
- Freshly milled pepper to taste

For the Chunk

- 1 cup sprouted adzuki, lentils, mung beans, or a combination (½ cup dry beans = 1 cup when sprouted. See sprouting directions p. 115.)
- ½ cup celery, finely chopped

- ½ cup sweet onion, finely chopped
- ½ cup cilantro, chopped, leaves only
- 1 avocado, coarsely chopped

Instructions for the Base

Soak 1 cup sun-dried tomatoes in 2 cups filtered water.

Blend all base ingredients, including soaking water from sun-dried tomatoes, in high-powered blender.

TO ASSEMBLE

Pour base ingredients from your blender over the vegetables and sprouted beans. Refrigerate overnight to blend flavors.

TO SERVE

Warm in the dehydrator at 110 degrees.

Ladle into bowls and top with sour cream (page 146) and a sprig of cilantro.

Tastes great served with cornbread (see recipe on page 97).

Macaroni and Cheese

SERVES 2

---

3 yellow zucchinis, squash, or yams

Slice zucchini in half lengthwise. With a melon baller, scoop out center seeds. Slice with mandolin slicer at medium thickness or use a knife. These half moon–shaped pieces will resemble macaroni noodles when covered with cheese.

Lightly salt and set aside.

Cheese

1½ cups cashews, soaked 4 hours

2 tablespoons of nutritional yeast (not raw)

2 tablespoons lemon juice

¾ cup water or more if needed

½ cup extra-virgin olive oil

1 clove garlic

1 tablespoon onion

1 tablespoon unpasteurized white miso or coconut aminos

Two generous pinches turmeric

Pinch or two paprika

Himalayan or Celtic sea salt to taste

Freshly milled pepper to taste

Blend all cheese ingredients in a high-powered blender until smooth. Start with half a cup water and add more if needed to make a smooth thick mixture. Taste for seasonings and adjust to your liking.

TO ASSEMBLE

Mix the macaroni noodles with desired amount of cheese.

Warm in dehydrator at 110 degrees for 1–5 hours or until noodles soften a bit and the cheese is warm.

Tip { Cheese sauce can be used on vegetables, including warmed broccoli or cauliflower.

Mike's Burger

MAKES APPROXIMATELY 12 PATTIES

For the Vegetables

2 cups sprouted kamut

2 cups walnuts

6–7 baby bella mushrooms

½ onion, coarsely chopped

1 small red pepper, coarsely chopped

1 zucchini, coarsely chopped

1 carrot, coarsely chopped

Himalayan or Celtic sea salt to taste

Freshly milled pepper to taste

Process sprouted kamut in your juicer with homogenizer blade or food processor; remove to a large mixing bowl.

Pulse-chop walnuts in your food processor until fine, but not overprocessed. Place into mixing bowl. Pulse-chop mushrooms, onion, red pepper, zucchini, and carrots until fine and place in mixing bowl.

For the Seeds

1 cup sunflower seeds

1 cup pumpkin seeds

Juice of ½ lemon

3–4 cloves of garlic

½ cup water

Himalayan or Celtic sea salt to taste

Freshly milled pepper to taste

Blend in high-powered blender adding water slowly as needed to make a smooth, thick paste. Remove and place in mixing bowl with the vegetables.

Additional Herbs

1 tablespoon coconut aminos, tamari, nama shoyu, or Bragg's

1 tablespoon basil, chopped

1 tablespoon Italian herbs

Add additional herbs of choice

TO ASSEMBLE

Add additional herbs to the mixing bowl.

Mix all ingredients in the bowl using hands if necessary to make sure everything is well incorporated. Taste for seasonings and adjust.

Make desired-size patties ¼ to ½ inch thick. Place on 3 nonstick dehydrator sheets.

Dehydrate for 3 hours at 105–110 degrees, then flip over onto mesh sheet and continue drying for another 2–4 hours. They should be dry on the outside and slightly soft in the inside.

TO SERVE

I prefer 2 romaine lettuce leaves, facing opposite directions, for my "bread." Mike likes iceberg lettuce leaves.

Place lettuce leaves on chopping board. If using romaine, cut a small piece off the hard part, overlapping lettuce lengthwise. If using iceberg, remove whole leaves by cutting out stem and setting in a bowl of ice water for ½ hour or more to loosen the leaves. Use 2 or 3 whole leaves as the "bread."

Place some Secret Sauce Dressing (see recipe on page 137) on the lettuce leaves. Place warm patty on the leaf and top with 1–2 slices of avocado, 1 slice tomato, 1 long-cut slice cucumber, 1 basil leaf, and a piece of thinly sliced onion. Fold over the lettuce like a sandwich.

Place the burger on a plate with a side of pickles (page 62).

Crabless Cakes and Tartar Sauce

MAKES 5-6 CAKES

1½ cups walnuts, soaked for 4 hours

½ cup sunflower seeds, ground in spice or coffee grinder

½ cup pumpkin seeds, ground in spice or coffee grinder

1 tablespoon flaxseed, ground into a very fine powder

½ cup yams, use shredding tool of food processor or large hand grater

1 cup zucchini, use shredding tool of food processor, or large hand grater

1 cup carrot, use shredding tool of food processor, or large hand grater

1 clove garlic, minced or crushed

2 tablespoons red pepper, finely chopped

2 tablespoons onion, finely chopped

2 tablespoons capers

1 tablespoon dill, finely chopped

1 tablespoon parsley, finely chopped

¼ cup seaweed, hijiki, dulse, or arame, soaked and drained well

1 teaspoon seafood mix (p. 59)

1 tablespoon extra-virgin olive oil

1 tablespoon lime juice

2 tablespoons lemon juice

½ teaspoon dry or Dijon mustard, or make your own (see recipe on p. 61)

2 tablespoons mayonnaise (see recipe on p. 61)

1 tablespoon nutritional yeast

½ teaspoon Himalayan or Celtic sea salt or to taste

Freshly milled pepper to taste

Tartar sauce (recipe follows)

Drain walnuts and grind in spice or coffee grinder. Place in mixing bowl.

Place ground sunflower meal in mixing bowl.

Squeeze water from shredded zucchini and place in mixing bowl.

In a food processor, place yams, carrots, and garlic. Pulse-chop until incorporated and still slightly chunky. Add balance of ingredients except walnuts, zucchini, and sunflower meal, pulsing until you reach a small crumbly mixture. Remove to mixing bowl.

Toss all ingredients in the bowl lightly to incorporate. Taste for salt and pepper and adjust if necessary.

Make patties ¾–1" thick and place on nonstick dehydrator sheets. Dehydrate for 3 hours at 105, then flip over and dehydrate approximately another 2–3 hours. They should be soft in the center with a very thin crust on the outside.

TO SERVE
Serve patties with a generous serving of tartar sauce and lemon wedge.

TARTAR SAUCE

½ cup cashews, soaked for 4 hours

Juice from ½ lemon

Water as needed

2 tablespoon capers (1 tablespoon chopped, the other left whole)

2 tablespoons celery, finely chopped

1 tablespoon onion, finely chopped

1 tablespoon dill, finely chopped

¾ tablespoon fresh horseradish, grated or prepared, to taste

Himalayan or Celtic sea salt to taste

Freshly milled pepper to taste

In food processor, place drained cashews, lemon, and water as needed and pulse-chop to make a thick blend. Remove and place in a mixing bowl. Add all ingredients to the cashew mixture and blend well by hand. Taste for seasonings and adjust. Best made a day ahead so all the seasonings meld.

Falafel

1 cup zucchini, coarsely chopped, or 1 cup sprouted garbanzo beans

½ cup of portobello mushroom, chopped

3 tablespoons parsley, finely chopped

2 tablespoons cilantro, finely chopped

½ small onion, chopped

1 teaspoon cumin

½ teaspoon coriander

2 cloves garlic, minced

Juice of ½ lemon

2 tablespoons extra-virgin olive oil

½ cup walnuts

½ cup pumpkin seed, ground into a meal in spice or coffee grinder

½ cup sunflower seed, ground into a meal in spice or coffee grinder

⅓ cup flaxseed, ground in spice or coffee grinder

A generous pinch of Himalayan or Celtic sea salt

Freshly milled black pepper to taste

Marinate chopped mushroom in coconut aminos or tamari and olive oil for 10–15 minutes.

Place all ingredients except flax meal in food processor. Pulse-chop until completely broken down and all ingredients are incorporated. Stop and scrape sides of the bowl as needed. Add water a tablespoon at a time if needed to help mixture hold together.

Using a heaping teaspoonful of mixture, place into the palm of your hand and form into a ball. Coat with ground flax meal and place balls on nonstick dehydrator sheet and dehydrate for 3 hours at 110 degrees. Remove the balls to the mesh screen and dehydrate another 3–5 hours until crust forms and there is a slight give to the center.

Spinach Quiche

MAKES 4 SMALL OR 1 LARGE PIE

Greek spinach pie (spanakopita) is stuffed with spinach, onion, herbs, and cheeses. The bottom and top layers of the pie consists of very thin layers of phyllo dough. I've adapted this classic dish into a raw quiche pie.

Small individual tart pans with removable bottoms work best as they dry faster in the dehydrator and look beautiful when served. If you do not have tart pans, line a pie tin or muffin tin with clear kitchen wrap before pressing in crust. I think tart pans are a good investment, as nothing looks more professional and beautiful than a pleated shell when the pan is removed.

For the Crust

1 cup macadamia nuts	1 tablespoon nutritional yeast (not raw)
½ cup cashews	1 teaspoon extra-virgin olive oil
2 tablespoons flaxseed (ground fine in spice or clean coffee grinder)	1 teaspoon lemon juice
1 clove garlic, crushed	Pinch of salt
¼ cup zucchini, coarsely chopped	1 tablespoon or more water if needed to make the crust sticky
1 tablespoon basil, chopped	

Place all ingredients into a food processor, reserving the water. Pulse until nuts are broken down. Add water slowly as needed. Pinch to see if mixture sticks together.

Use coconut oil to grease tart pans. Divide mixture into 4 portions. Press crust into pans using wet hands if necessary.

Place tart pans on the mesh dehydrator tray and dehydrate at 110–115 degrees for 2 hours or until the crust is firm enough to lift from the pan. Gently set crusts on mesh sheet and continue dehydrating for 6–8 hours more.

Spinach Filling

½ cup pine nuts (reserve to sprinkle on the crust before filling)	½ cup onion, chopped
1½ cups cashews, soaked for 4 hours or use cashew nut cheese	1 teaspoon dill, finely chopped
(see recipe on p. 146.)	1 clove garlic, minced
1 tablespoon nutritional yeast (not raw)	2 cups spinach, tightly packed
1 tablespoon lemon juice	1½ cups mushrooms, wiped clean and chopped
Pinch of Himalayan or Celtic sea salt	1 tablespoon basil, chopped
1 cup zucchini, chopped	2 Roma tomatoes, seeded and finely chopped
1 tablespoon, tamari, white miso, nama shoyu or Bragg's	

Marinate mushrooms in 1 teaspoon tamari, nama shoyu, or Bragg's for 10 minutes. Drain.

In a high-powered blender add cashews, nutritional yeast, lemon juice, and salt. Add ½ cup water using more if needed to make a very thick, smooth cheese sauce.

When smooth, move to a large mixing bowl.

Place zucchini, tamari, onion, dill, garlic in food processor and grind until smooth. Add to bowl with cashew mixture.

Coarsely chop spinach in food processor or by hand. Add to bowl.

Mix all ingredients until well incorporated.

Sprinkle pine nuts on the bottom of the crusts and fill to the top with the spinach mixture.

Dehydrate 24 hours or until centers are set. Test by lightly shaking or stick a toothpick in the center. As quiches cool, they continue to set.

TO SERVE
Place on individual plates, top with mini colored heirloom tomatoes that have been cut in half and marinated in olive oil, garlic, salt, and pepper for 10–15 minutes or more. Garnish with a sprig of basil.

Tip  Serve with a simple salad.

Stuffed Grape Leaves

SERVES 4

1 jar grape leaves in brine, rinsed, or 1 bunch of chard leaves, stemmed

2 cups sprouted wild rice (see page 170 for sprouting methods)

1 cup walnuts, chopped till crumbly

2 cloves garlic, crushed

½ cup scallions, chopped

Generous pinch of salt and pepper

1 tablespoon mint, chopped

2 tablespoons lemon juice

6–7 tablespoons pine nuts

2 tablespoons raisins

Place ¾ sprouted rice in food processor with nuts, garlic, scallions, salt, mint, and lemon juice. Pulse-chop 5–6 times. Remove to bowl and add remaining unprocessed ¼ rice, raisins, and pine nuts. Blend together.

If using a chard leaf, remove the stem. If they are too large, cut leaf in half. You want them to resemble the size of stuffed grape leaves when finished.

If using grape leaves and they are small, use two leaves and overlap so they will hold the filling.

Place a heaping tablespoon or more of the filling on to the leaf. From the side closest to you, roll leaf over, filling one roll, then fold in the sides and continue rolling up tightly.

If you have a bamboo steamer or vegetable steamer, line one layer deep, with grape or collard leaves, and place rolls seam-side down on leaves.

When all leaves are placed seam-side down, generously squeeze lemon on top and brush with olive oil. Place steamer on top of baking dish partially filled with water and several lemon slices or juiced rinds. Cover with foil to steam. Set dehydrator temperature at 110 degrees and dehydrate for 4 hours. When finished, leaves will be softened.

If using your oven, place on lowest degree with the door slightly ajar. Check to make sure the food does not cook and is only lightly steamed.

Serve warm or at room temperature with lemon wedges and tzaziki (see recipe on page 148).

Vegetable Patties

MAKES 8–9 PATTIES

5–6 carrots, juiced—reserve pulp for patties

1 apple, juiced—pulp reserved for patties

1 cup pumpkin seeds, ground in VitaMix, spice or coffee grinder

¾ cup sunflower seeds, ground in VitaMix, spice or coffee grinder

3–4 tablespoons lemon

2–3 cloves garlic

1 tablespoon unprocessed white miso, coconut aminos, or tamari

½ cup filtered water

½ cup hijiki, soaked and drained, or ¼ cup dulse flakes

¼–½ of medium onion, finely chopped

½ sweet red pepper, finely chopped

1 tablespoon capers

1 teaspoon mustard

1 teaspoon ocean seasonings—from herb and spice section

Pinch of Himalayan or Celtic sea salt

Freshly milled pepper

In a high-speed blender, place pumpkin meal, sunflower meal, lemon, garlic, and miso. Blend, adding water as needed to make a smooth, thick paste.

Place carrots and apple pulp in a mixing bowl and add seed mixture from the blender, along with hijiki, onion, red pepper, and salt and pepper to taste. Blend very well with a spatula or with your hands.

Make patties about ¼–½ inch thick and place on 2–3 nonstick dehydrator sheets. Brush tops with olive oil. Dehydrate for 2 hours, then flip onto mesh trays and dehydrate for another 2–3 hours. The finished patty should have a thin crust on the outside and be slightly soft in the middle.

TO SERVE
Top with fresh lemon juice and a sprinkle of capers, or secret sauce (see recipe on page 137).

Pizza

Some raw pizza crusts I've tasted were more crackerlike, and although they tasted good with all the toppings, I knew I wanted to try to duplicate the flour crust I made for years as a vegetarian. It took some time to get it to my liking, but now I can enjoy pizza and not miss out on this great dish. I admit, it's not quite the same as pizza in Italy, but this version is so much healthier and the taste is quite incredible.

3 cups sprouted buckwheat, ground in your blender or coffee grinder

¼ cup sunflower seeds, ground in your blender, spice or coffee grinder

¼ cup agave or sweetener of choice

2 cups zucchini, chopped, salted, wiped dry

3 tablespoons lecithin sunflower

2 tablespoons Irish moss gel (see product index, page 50)

6 tablespoons olive oil

2 cups springwater

1 teaspoon Celtic or Himalayan sea salt

3 tablespoons Italian Mix (page 58)

2 cloves garlic, chopped

¾ cup nutritional yeast (not raw but vegan)

1½ cups flax meal (ground flax seeds)

Put all ingredients in your blender except nutritional yeast and ground flaxseed. Blend until mixed well. Mixture will be too thick to add flax at this point, so remove it from the blender into a bowl and mix in ground flax by hand or use a food processor, pulsing until well incorporated. Divide mixture in half and pour each half onto a nonstick dehydrator sheet. Shape into a large squares or rounds, ½ to 1 inch thick, and raising the ends to resemble the crust of a pizza. A flat wet spatula works best to smooth out the mixture. Dehydrate for approximately 10 hours at 105–110. When top has a slight crust and the center is still soft, check to see if you can carefully slide the crust onto the mesh screen. Dehydrate for another 9 hours or until center section is still soft and outside has a thin crust. Check occasionally to make sure the crust is not drying out; the softness gives it the pizza-dough effect.

You can use pasta sauce (see recipe on page 187), pesto (see recipe on page 187), and any toppings you like, including basic cheese (see recipe on page 143), chopped olives, sliced mushrooms, red onion, capers, fresh tomato, sweet bell pepper, basil, and Italian herbs.

Pomodoro Lasagna

SERVES 5-6

Please don't let the list of ingredients put you off. The recipe is easy to make, and it goes together quicker than it looks. This is a delicious dish and well worth making. I actually find my raw version easier than making the cooked version from scratch.

For best results, plan this dish a couple days ahead so the cheese can ferment.

For the Noodles

3–4 large zucchinis

Peel and slice the zucchinis. For 4 layers, you will need 24 strips total. Use 6 strips for each layer, two rows of three lengthwise, slightly overlapping each other. If you need to feed several people, make 2–3 platters instead of all in one, making it easier to cut and serve into individual portions.

For the Cheese

1½ cups cashews, soaked 4 hours

4 tablespoons Irish moss gel (optional, but it works to harden the cheese to a nice consistency; see instructions on p. 50)

½ teaspoon probiotic powder (to help fermenting and curing process)

1 tablespoon of nutritional yeast (not raw)

1 teaspoon lemon juice

A good pinch or two of Himalayan sea salt

Filtered water as needed—approximately ¾ cup

Blend all ingredients in a high-powered blender until smooth. Start with ½-cup water and add more if needed to make a very smooth, thick mixture. Cheese can be used without fermenting, but the texture and taste is not quite as good. If you decide to use the cheese immediately, add an extra handful of nuts to thicken the cheese.

Place a strainer lined with cheesecloth over a bowl. Scrape cheese mixture into the cheesecloth and fold up the sides to cover the cheese. Place a plate on top of the cheese and a weight just heavy enough to slowly and gently push out the extra liquid. Leave on the kitchen counter for 24 hours to culture at room temperature.

Remove cheese from cloth and use immediately, or it can be stored in a covered container in the refrigerator for 5 days.

For the Pesto Layer

- 2 cups basil, tightly packed
- 1–2 cloves garlic, cut in half
- ½ cup walnuts or pine nuts, or ¼ cup of each
- Approximately 2–3 tablespoons of extra-virgin olive oil
- Generous pinch or two of Himalayan salt

Place nuts and garlic in your food processor and pulse until broken down but still in small pieces. Add basil and salt; pulse while slowly adding olive oil through the feed tube until smooth and creamy.

Taste for saltiness and adjust to taste.

Remove pesto to a mixing bowl.

(You do not have to rinse the food processor from the pesto residue to make the pasta sauce.)

For the Red Pasta Sauce Layer

- 2 cups tomatoes, cut in quarters
- 1½ cup sun-dried tomatoes, soaked for 1 hour or until soft
- 2 cloves garlic, cut in half
- 1 tablespoon tamari, nama shoyu, or Bragg's
- 1½ tablespoons of Italian herbs, consisting of thyme, rosemary, basil, marjoram, and oregano
- Good pinch or two of Himalayan salt
- Freshly milled pepper

If you like a little spice, add a pinch of dried chilies or a tiny piece of jalapeño pepper.

Place the sun-dried tomatoes in your food processor and pulse a few times to break down slightly; add the fresh tomatoes, garlic, tamari, salt, pepper, and herbs. Pulse until well combined. The sauce should be thick and slightly chunky.

Optional: but adds great taste between layers: raw olives sliced or chopped, capers, and very thinly sliced portobello mushrooms marinated in tamari and olive oil.

Tip { Lasagna consists of four layers of noodles. Use a flat, long plate that fits in dehydrator. This recipe will make two platters of lasagna 4 inches wide and about 10 inches long. Don't use a conventional lasagna baking dish, as it's harder to remove the portions. If you do not have a dehydrator, an oven on the lowest degree with the door ajar will do. Be careful not to overheat.

TO ASSEMBLE

1. Place a thin layer of red sauce on the bottom of the plate. Overlap slices of noodles to desired width and length. Top noodles with dollops of cheese. Sprinkle raw sliced black olives and capers over the top of the cheese.

2. Place second layer of noodles on top and lightly press down. Top this layer with pesto spread to cover the zucchini slices.

3. Place third layer of noodles on top and lightly press down. Top this layer with more cheese and add drained marinated portobello mushrooms.

4. Place fourth layer on noodles on top and lightly press down and cover this layer with a generous amount of red sauce.

To top lasagna, cut 1½ cups heirloom cherry tomatoes in half. Marinate 15 minutes in 1 clove crushed garlic, a few dashes of olive oil, ribbon-cut basil, salt and pepper, and mix lightly to incorporate flavors. Place mixture on top of lasagna with extra sliced basil.

Make Parmesan nut cheese by putting a generous handful of cashews (not soaked) in your food processor; add 1 clove garlic and a generous pinch or two of salt. Pulse until it looks like Parmesan cheese. Sprinkle on top of lasagna.

Preheat dehydrator to 110 degrees. Remove unnecessary shelves and place the lasagna plates on remaining shelves. Heat for 1–3 hours or until lasagna is warmed through.

TO SERVE

Cut with a very sharp knife and make individual servings. Decorate the plate with a teaspoon of pine nuts, capers, and chopped basil. Serve immediately.

Pasta alla Checca

SERVES 2

One of my favorite Italian foods is simple pasta. One of my favorite kitchen tools is my spiral slicer. It turns zucchini into pasta noodles that not only look like the real thing, but taste like the real thing, especially when topped with traditional Italian checca.

Pasta alla Checca is a dish created in Italy and served in the summer months when tomatoes are at their peak. It consists of uncooked tomatoes and simple Italian herbs, and the outcome is molto bono *(translated means "very good")!*

Enjoy this zucchini pasta with a variety of sauces.

3 large zucchinis

4–5 tomatoes, seeded and diced, or heirloom cherry tomatoes

1 clove garlic, minced

½ cup raw olives, coarsely chopped

2 tablespoons capers

20 fresh basil leaves, ribbon-sliced or torn

½ cup extra-virgin olive oil

Cashew nut Parmesan cheese

Himalayan salt to taste

Freshly milled black pepper

Peel zucchinis or leave skin on. It resembles actual pasta without the skin; however, the green color is appealing to the eyes, so it's your choice.

Spiralize zucchinis, or if you do not own this kitchen tool, use a potato peeler and make long flat fettuccini-type noodles. Put a pinch of salt on zucchini, toss, and let rest for 15–30 minutes.

Meanwhile, combine tomatoes, garlic, olives, capers, olive oil, salt and pepper to taste, reserving the basil. Let mixture rest at room temperature for 30 minutes to meld seasonings.

Using a paper or kitchen towel, gently squeeze pasta to extract all liquid. Place in a large mixing bowl. Put half the checca mixture into the bowl, along with ¾ of the basil, and gently toss.

TO SERVE
Use individual mold to stack the pasta high on the plates (I use an empty can with both sides removed) or divide into bowls. Top with the balance of checca mixture, sprinkle on Parmesan nut cheese, and top with chopped reserved basil. Bellissima!

Sweet Potato Gnocchi

SERVES 2

Gnocchi is an Italian specialty made with flour, eggs, and starchy potatoes. My raw version, though not authentic, satisfies my palate and of course is a much-healthier version.

Gnocchi can be served with a variety of sauces, including olive oil and sage, nut cream, red pasta sauce, or pesto. This particular recipe will have a rather simple flavorful sauce, which brings out the flavor of the gnocchis.

2 cups jicama

2 cups sweet potato or yam

1 cup basic cheese (see recipe on p. 143) or 1 cup sunflower seeds and 1 cup pumpkin seeds

¼ cup Irish moss paste

2 tablespoons nutritional yeast

1 teaspoon Himalayan salt to taste

Freshly milled pepper

Filtered water as needed

If using sunflower and pumpkin seeds, grind sunflower and pumpkin seeds in high-powered blender, add juice from ½ lemon, and ½ cup or more water to make a smooth, thick paste.

Place jicama and sweet potatoes in food processor and pulse until smooth. Remove from processor and place mixture in high-powered blender. Using plunger tool, continue to blend until mixture is very smooth. Place mixture in filter bag or cheesecloth and squeeze out all the liquid. Mixture should be dry but still soft. Place into a bowl and add cheese mixture, Irish moss paste, and nutritional yeast, incorporating well. Taste for seasonings and add more salt if necessary.

Use a teaspoon and place mixture into the palm of your hand. Shape gnocchis so they are small ovals and, using the tine of a fork, press lightly to make fork lines. Place gnocchis on nonstick dehydrator sheet and dehydrate approximately 4 hours. Finished gnocchi will be soft inside with a light crust on the outside. Eating warm is best.

For the Sauce

½ cup extra-virgin olive oil

1 clove garlic, minced

Leaves from 4 stems sage, approximately 12 leaves, chopped

Himalayan salt to taste, best a little salty

Freshly milled pepper

Chopped basil

Capers, to garnish

Place all ingredients in a bowl and combine. Place bowl in dehydrator to warm and meld ingredients.

TO SERVE

I like to warm my plates in the dehydrator or oven so the gnocchi stays warm when served. Divide on two serving plates and spoon over the sauce. Top with chopped basil and capers.

Stuffed Portobello Mushroom with Basil Pesto

SERVES 2

A beautiful presentation for company, and the preparation is deliciously quick. The only time spent is when the mushrooms are in the dehydrator warming up.

Mushrooms will be plump, juicy, and tender after they are heated. If you don't have a dehydrator, set oven on the lowest heat and leave the door open. The thing to remember is to keep the enzymes and nutrients intact; internal temperature should not be over 115 degrees.

If using this dish as a starter course, use baby portobellos and allow 1–2 per person.

2 large portobello mushrooms—or 6–8 baby portobellos

4 tablespoons tamari or nama shoyu

2 tablespoons extra-virgin olive oil

1 recipe basil pesto (see recipe, p. 187)

With a damp paper towel, clean off the mushroom cap and remove the stem.

Trim the bottom of the removed stem piece and cut lengthwise in half. Marinate mushroom caps and stems in 3 tablespoons olive oil and 2 tablespoons of tamari or nama shoyu. Turn mushrooms over to coat them well with the oil mixture; if more is needed, sprinkle directly onto mushrooms.

Choose two small salad plates that will fit into your dehydrator shelf. Or if using baby portobellos, use a baking dish. Place one mushroom filling-side up on each plate, reserving remaining marinade. Fill mushroom caps with approximately 2 tablespoons pesto mixture, smoothing out as you go. Place the marinated stems on the plate.

Add a thin slice of tomato or fresh chopped tomatoes to top the pesto. Pour the reserved marinade mixture on top, or if none is left, put a dash of tamari or nama shoyu on top.

Put the dishes on two dehydrator trays and dehydrate at 110 degrees for 1–2 hours, depending how thick the mushrooms are. You can tell the mushroom is done when the outside rim turns dark and has a slightly cooked look.

When ready to serve, squeeze fresh lemon on top.

Portobello Mushroom Stew

SERVES 4

3 large portobello mushrooms

½ medium onion, finely chopped

6 tablespoons pesto (see recipe on page 187)

6 tablespoons basic nut cheese (see recipe on page 143) or 1 cup of quick cheese version, opposite

2 medium tomatoes, chopped

½ cup raw olives, chopped

¼ cup capers

3 tablespoons extra-virgin olive oil

2 tablespoons coconut aminos, tamari, nama shoyu, or Bragg's

Pine nuts, for serving

Chopped parsley, for garnish

Wipe mushroom caps with a slightly damp cloth or paper towel. Remove stem and cut cap in thirds and then thirds again. Place slices in glass baking dish and marinate with olive oil and tamari for 15 minutes, turning twice.

Remove mushroom slices to a plate and place the chopped onion in glass baking dish that will fit into dehydrator. Lay mushroom slices over the onions, and spoon cheese and pesto over the top. Sprinkle with chopped tomatoes, olives, and capers.

Dehydrate for 2–3 hours at 110 degrees until the mushrooms slightly soften and the pesto and cheese melt in. If you want a crunch to your stew after dehydration, add the following vegetables:

¼ cup carrots, sliced into thin rounds

¼ cup celery, finely chopped

¼ cup red bell pepper, sliced into thin strips

¼ cup zucchini, sliced into thin rounds and cut in half

¼ cup tomatoes, chopped

Heat for additional 20 minutes.

TO SERVE

Plate and sprinkle with pine nuts. Garnish with chopped flat-leaf parsley.

QUICK CASHEW CHEESE

1 cup cashews

¾ cup water or more if needed

1 tablespoon lemon, juiced

3 tablespoons nutritional yeast

Himalayan or Celtic sea salt to taste

Freshly milled pepper

Place all ingredients in a high-speed blender and blend until smooth.

Shiitake Mushroom Skewers

SERVES 4

12 small shiitake mushrooms, wiped clean with a damp cloth, stems removed

6 enoki mushrooms, depending on their size—you will need 24 pieces, 2 inches long

4 tablespoons coconut aminos or tamari

⅛ teaspoon extra-virgin olive oil

1 tablespoon agave or maple syrup

Daikon radish, shredded

Small piece of ginger, grated

Mix coconut aminos or tamari and sweetener together with a whisk.

Cut the enoki into 2-inch pieces.

Marinate both mushrooms for 15–30 minutes in coconut aminos, oil, and agave, turning to coat a few times.

Spear one piece of enoki stem vertically onto a wooden skewer, followed by a shiitake and then another piece of vertically speared enoki. Continue making 12 skewers.

Place all skewers onto nonstick sheets of dehydrator trays and dehydrate for 30 minutes to 1 hour at 105 degrees.

Check after 30 minutes and remove if mushrooms feel wilted and cooked. You can test by sticking a toothpick in them.

Mix daikon and grated ginger together.

TO SERVE

Place 2 skewers on each plate and drizzle some of the marinade sauce around the plate. Top with a teaspoon-size round of shredded daikon and grated ginger in the center of the two spears.

Enchilada

SERVES 4

For tortillas (see recipe on page 153)

Filling

4 Tortillas	1 ear of corn, cut off the cob
1 zucchini, finely chopped	4 scallions, chopped
1 small red onion, finely chopped	½ cup raw olives, coarsely chopped
1 red pepper, finely chopped	

Set tortillas aside.

Place all ingredients, except scallions and black olives, into a baking dish. Pour 2 tablespoons of oil over top of vegetables. Add salt and pepper, 1 tablespoon water, and lightly mix to coat vegetables. Cover with foil and place the dish in the dehydrator to soften approximately 3 hours.

SALSA

2 tomatoes, seeded and finely chopped	1 small piece Serrano or jalapeño chili, finely chopped
¼ small onion, finely chopped	1 tablespoon lime juice
½ piece garlic, finely minced	A dash of cumin
½ cup cilantro, chopped	Salt and pepper to taste

TOPPINGS
1 avocado, chopped
3 scallions, chopped
Salsa
Cashew sour cream (see recipe on page 146)

TO ASSEMBLE
Place one tortilla on a chopping board. Fill with a tablespoon or two of the vegetable filling mixture. Add a sprinkle of scallions and chopped olives and a line of sour cream. Roll up, placing seam-side down, in a glass baking dish. Cover and place back in dehydrator to warm all ingredients about 1 hour.

TO SERVE
Carefully remove each enchilada with a flat spatula onto warmed plates. Top enchilada with chopped avocado, salsa, scallions, and a drizzle of cashew sour cream.

Serve with sprouted Mexican rice (see recipe on page 170) and a light green salad.

Fajitas

Cooked fajitas are a combination of sautéed vegetables served on a sizzling platter with a side of corn or flour tortillas. This lighter raw version comes wrapped in a collard leaf or raw tortilla (see recipe on page 153).

1 zucchini, thinly sliced, salted, and placed on paper towel to drain

1 red pepper, seeded and thinly sliced

¼ small onion, thinly sliced

1 tomato, thinly sliced and pieces cut in half

5 button mushrooms, stemmed and thinly sliced

Large collard leaves, stems removed

For the Marinade

2 tablespoons extra-virgin olive oil

1 tablespoon coconut aminos or tamari

1 tablespoon lemon juice

Freshly milled pepper

⅛ teaspoon cumin

1 clove garlic, crushed

A sprinkle of chili flakes

A squirt of agave or sweetener of choice

Mix together with vegetables and marinate for 30 minutes or longer, adjusting seasonings to taste.

If preferred, place marinated vegetables in a glass baking dish and cover with foil. Warm in dehydrator for 2 hours. Add 2 tablespoons filtered water to steam.

TO ASSEMBLE:

Lay collard leaf on a cutting board and gently cut out stem. Spoon vegetables about 2 inches from end closest to you. Fold end over filling and roll up. Place on a plate seam-side down. If you are using tortillas, it's best to plate individual serving with filling and tortillas and let each person prepare their own.

Tip { Avocado, scallions, salsa, or sour cream are excellent additions to these fajitas.

Thai Pasta

SERVES 2

For the Noodles

2 large yellow zucchinis, peeled and spiralized

1 parsnip, sprialized

1 red bell pepper, cut into thin strips

1 carrot, shredded

2 small firm cucumber pickles, peeled

2 green onions, chopped

2 tablespoons sesame seeds

8 basil leaves, ribbon cut

½ cup cilantro leaves, loosely packed and coarsely chopped

Use spiralizer or peeler to make the zucchini and parsnip into noodles. If using a spiralizer, cut zucchini in half to make shorter noodles. Julienne-cut cucumber. Place cucumber in a bowl and lightly salt mix and let sit until wilted about 1 hour. After 1 hour, press all water out of zucchini and cucumbers with a clean kitchen or paper towel. Place all pasta ingredients in a large salad bowl.

For the Dressing

1½ cups cashews, soaked for 4 hours

1 cup coconut water

½ cup basil leaves

1 tablespoon sesame seeds

¼ cup agave or sweetener of choice

1 clove garlic, cut in half

1 tablespoon apple cider vinegar

1 teaspoon coconut aminos, tamari, nama shoyu, or Bragg's

½ teaspoon fresh ginger, grated, or ⅛ teaspoon powdered

1 small piece jalapeño pepper, minced, or a pinch of chili flakes

Freshly milled pepper to taste

Himalayan sea salt if needed to taste

Place all ingredients into high-powered blender and blend until smooth, adding water as needed. Taste for seasonings and adjust. Look for a creamy texture without lumps.

Place pasta into a large bowl and pour half the dressing, tossing gently. Add more and gently toss.

TO SERVE

For a decorative serving, place a can with both ends removed on a serving plate. Pack the pasta in and gently press down to compact the noodles. Slowly lift can, leaving a tall tower on the plate. Top with a sprinkle of pine nuts, some whole cilantro leaves, and a long strip or two of chives.

Warm Asian Noodles

SERVES 2–4

3–4 zucchini, peeled and spiralized

1½ cups warm water

1 clove garlic

4 tablespoons coconut aminos or white miso paste

2 tablespoons extra-virgin olive oil

½ teaspoon sesame seeds

½" ginger, peeled and grated

1 tablespoon raw peanut butter or sesame tahini

⅛ teaspoon paprika

Pinch of chili flakes

Freshly milled pepper

Dash of rice vinegar

1 tablespoon agave, or sweetener of choice

1 cup shiitake mushrooms, sliced, with stems removed

1 tablespoon dulse flakes

½ cup chives, chopped

3 tablespoons daikon or radish, chopped

3 green onions, chopped

1 cup bean sprouts

Place sliced shiitake mushrooms in a bowl, drizzle on olive oil and tamari, mix, and let rest for 10–15 minutes.

Spiralize zucchini or use potato peeler to make into flat noodles. Lightly salt and set aside.

Place water in a pot on the stove and warm gently. Do not boil or overheat. Place warm water into your blender and add garlic, miso, oil, sesame seeds, ginger, peanut butter, paprika, chili flakes, vinegar, and agave. Blend until smooth. Taste for seasonings and adjust.

Drain zucchini noodles and place in a large bowl. Add shiitake mushrooms, including marinade, dulse, chives, daikon, green onions, and sprouts. Toss gently to incorporate all ingredients. Noodles can be heated lightly on the stove. Do not cook or overheat to keep it raw.

TO SERVE
Divide into bowls and garnish with chopped chives and a sprinkle of sesame seeds. Serve with chopstick.

CHAPTER 12

·····················

sweets

·····················

Sweet

Being a raw foodist does not mean you have to give up sweets. I consider them a treat and find satisfaction in small amounts. I've always been a chocolate lover, and I still am. I enjoy raw treats much better than standard deserts, and they are certainly much healthier than sugar-laden processed deserts. Don't deprive yourself, but remember, moderation is always best.

Vanilla Ice Cream

3 cups young Thai coconut water (if not available, you can buy coconut water at your health food store) or 3 cups almond milk and ½ cup cashews soaked for 4 hours

¾ cup raw agave

6 tablespoons coconut oil, melted in a double boiler

Scrape seeds from 2 vanilla beans or use 1 teaspoon vanilla extract

Place all ingredients in a high-powered blender except coconut oil. Blend until completely smooth. Slowly pour in melted coconut oil while blender is running and blend a few more minutes.

Pour the mixture into a glass jar with a lid and store overnight in the refrigerator, or no less than 6 hours.

If using a commercial ice cream maker, follow manufacturer's directions. If you do not own an ice cream maker, put the liquid into a glass baking dish and place in freezer. Let ice cream firm up enough to scoop out. Raw ice cream gets hard when frozen, and 10 minutes out of the freezer is enough to soften it.

Tip { Blend in flesh from 1 Thai young coconut.

Chocolate Ice Cream

3 cups Thai young coconut water (fresh is best, but you can buy coconut water at health food stores) or 3 cups almond milk with ½ cup cashews soaked for 4 hours

¾ cup raw agave

6 tablespoons coconut oil, melted

Scrape seeds from 1 vanilla bean or use 1 teaspoon vanilla extract

⅓ cup cacao powder

1 tablespoon cacao nibs (optional)

Place all ingredients in a high-powered blender except coconut oil. Blend until completely smooth. Slowly pour in melted coconut oil while blender is running. Blend a few more minutes. Taste for sweetness and add more if needed to your taste.

Pour the mixture into a glass jar with a lid and store overnight in the refrigerator, or no less than 6 hours.

If using a commercial ice cream maker, follow manufacturer's directions. If you do not own an ice cream maker, put the liquid into a glass baking dish and place in freezer. Let ice cream firm up enough to scoop out. Raw ice cream gets hard when frozen, and 10 minutes out of the freezer is enough to soften it.

Tip { With either the coconut water or almond milk, add meat from one Thai young coconut. Chocolate ice cream can also be made from Hot Chocolate Only Better. (See recipe on page 77.)

Strawberry Ice Cream

3 cups Thai young coconut water (fresh is best; if not, you can buy coconut water at your health food store)

Or replace coconut water with the following:

3 cups almond milk (see recipe on p. 74) with ½ cup cashews soaked for 4 hours

¾ cup raw agave

6 tablespoons coconut oil, melted

Scrape seeds from 1 vanilla bean or 1 use teaspoon vanilla extract

4 cups fresh strawberries

Place all ingredients in a high-powered blender except coconut oil. Blend until completely smooth. Slowly pour in melted coconut oil while blender is running. Blend a few more minutes. Taste for sweetness. Use more sweetener if necessary.

Pour the mixture into a glass jar with a lid and store overnight in the refrigerator, or no less than 6 hours.

If using a commercial ice cream maker, follow manufacturer's directions. If you do not own an ice cream maker, put the liquid into a glass baking dish and place in freezer. Let ice cream firm up enough to scoop out. Raw ice cream gets hard when frozen, and 10 minutes out of the freezer is enough to soften it.

Tip { With either the coconut water or almond milk, add meat from one Thai young coconut.

Almond Cookie

1 cup almonds, soaked overnight and dried in dehydrator for 4 hours

2 tablespoons agave or sweetener of choice

1 tablespoon fine dried coconut

¼ teaspoon vanilla

4 medjool dates, soaked until soft, and drained

½ cup pine nuts

Pinch of salt

¼ teaspoon maple extract

¼ cup almond butter

Grind almonds in blender, spice or coffee grinder until a fine meal.

Place all ingredients in food processor except ⅓ almond meal and pine nuts. Process until smooth, scraping down sides as needed. Blend in pine nuts by hand.

Dough will be very sticky and soft. Sprinkle remaining almond flour on a pastry or chopping board and knead flour in. Place in refrigerator to chill for 5 hours or overnight.

When dough is firm, place on chopping board and roll out ¼ to ½ inches thick with almond-floured rolling pin. Cut with cookie cutter or shape by hand. Place cookies on mesh screen of dehydrator tray and dehydrate for 10 hours at 110 degrees. No need to turn. Test for doneness; they should be crunchy on the outside and softer in the middle.

Simple Cacao Chocolate

Will make approximately 2 cups

1¾ cacao butter

1 vanilla bean (do not use extract)

½ cup maple sugar powder or sucanat granules ground very fine in spice grinder

¾ cup cacao powder

1 tablespoon agave

Melt cacao butter in a double boiler. Scrape seeds from vanilla bean and incorporate with the melting cacao butter.

In a large bowl, add cacao powder, melted cacao butter, salt, and powdered sweetener (do not add liquid sweetener or agave at this time).

Use a wire whisk and blend together until very smooth and all lumps are gone.

When smooth, taste for sweetness. Add agave or powdered sweetener to suit your taste; bitter chocolate or sweet, it's up to you.

Use for dipping, or pour into candy molds, or line a small glass baking dish with parchment paper and pour the extra chocolate on top. Press chopped pecans or almond into the chocolate and place in freezer. Break into pieces to serve.

Candy can be stored in refrigerator or freezer.

Tip { Use this chocolate for dipping anything from cookies to fruit.

Ice Cream Sandwich

Use almond cookie recipe opposite.

Make any flavor ice cream (see ice cream recipes).

Place 1 cookie on a piece of plastic kitchen wrap. Mound ice cream on top and press down while placing another cookie on top. Smooth out the sides of the ice cream and roll the sides in any of the following: coconut, cacao powder, chopped nuts, or dip into chocolate. Wrap sandwich in plastic wrap and place in the freezer until hard. To serve, take out of the freezer 10 minutes before serving.

Tip { Give each person their own cacao chocolate dipping bowl to dip as they eat.

Chocolate-Covered Nutty Candy

1 cup fine coconut

1 cup coarse coconut

¼ cup cacao nibs

1 tablespoon vanilla

Pinch of salt

1 cup pecans

½ cup dates, soaked

4 tablespoon coconut oil, melted

1¾ cacao butter

1 vanilla bean (do not use extract)

½ cup maple sugar powder or sucanat granules ground very fine in spice grinder

¾ cup cacao powder

1 tablespoon agave

In food processor:

Chop nuts into small chunks. Add dates one at a time and pulse-chop 4–5 times.

Place mixture in a mixing bowl.

In food processor (you do not have to clean after chopping nuts):

Pulse-chop 3–4 times coconut, cacao nibs, vanilla, and salt. Place in bowl with nuts.

Blend mixture together very well.

Using a teaspoon, make small oval-shaped candies and place on nonstick paper. Place in freezer to harden. Prepare Simple Cacao Chocolate (see p. 202).

Line a baking sheet with parchment paper or nonstick dehydrator sheet. Remove nut/coconut candies from freezer. Stick a toothpick or longer wood skewer in nut mixture and dip one at a time into chocolate. Let extra chocolate drip back into the bowl, then place dipped candy on parchment paper or sheet. Put back in freezer to set.

Chocolate-Covered Treats

Prepare Simple Cacao Chocolate (see p. 202) Peel bananas, cut off about an inch at one end or, if banana is large, cut in half. Stick an ice cream stick in the cut end and freeze on a baking sheet lined with parchment, waxed paper, or nonstick dehydrator sheet. When frozen, place in a ziplock bag. Freezing this way keeps the bananas from sticking together. Remove bananas from freezer and dip one at a time into the chocolate, making sure to cover the whole banana. Place on parchment or nonstick paper and place back in freezer.

Macaroons

1 cup flaked coconut	½ cup agave or sweetener of choice
1 cup large coconut pieces	2 tablespoons coconut butter, melted in double boiler (preferred to coconut oil)
¾ cup raw almonds ground into a meal, or flour	½ teaspoon vanilla
⅛ teaspoon salt	1 teaspoon almond extract

In food processor:

Put coconut, almond meal, and salt. Pulse-chop 4–5 times. Add remaining ingredients, pulsing until incorporated.

Place a teaspoon of mixture into your palms and roll into a ball; place on nonstick dehydrator sheet and press down lightly to flatten or shape as you like.

Dehydrate at 110 degrees for 8 hours. They will still be soft, but firm up when refrigerated or frozen.

Tip { To give the macaroons a baked look, place 1 teaspoon cinnamon in a bowl, add water, and make into a smooth liquid. Brush macaroons with cinnamon mixture and let dry in refrigerator. Dip half the macaroon in cacao chocolate. (See chocolate recipe, p. 202.)

Chia Pudding

SERVES 2

Chia seeds are another miracle food because of their nonmarine whole-food source of omega-3 and dietary fiber. Omega-3 fatty acids can normalize blood pressure, help lower bad cholesterol levels, help to strengthen muscles and bones, and are good for digestion.

Chia seeds? Chia Pet? Yes, the same chia seeds that are used to sprout green hair on animal-shaped terracotta figurines. When I was a little girl, I remember soaking seeds until they were gelatinous and then rubbing them into the grooves in the figurines. A hole in the center of the animal figure is where water was kept to keep the seeds moist. At the time, I never knew these seeds were edible and full of omega-3, fiber, and protein.

Basic recipe tastes like tapioca pudding.

2 cups almond milk (see recipe on p. 74)	⅔ cup chia seeds
1 tablespoon agave or sweetener of choice	2 teaspoons vanilla extract
⅛ teaspoon cinnamon if desired	

Soak chia seeds in almond milk. Mix well and let rest 15 minutes. Stir with a fork to break up any lumps and let rest another 10 minutes. Add agave and vanilla and stir in until well blended. Mixture will firm up overnight in refrigerator.

 Tip { Toss in berries, add a dash of maple extract, use coconut water from a young Thai coconut. Add cacao powder and sweetener to taste.

Banana Pudding

SERVES 1

1 cup almond milk (see recipe on p. 74)	1 tablespoon agave or sweetener of choice
⅓ cup chia seeds	1 teaspoon vanilla extract
1 ripe banana, mashed	

Soak chia seeds in 1 cup of almond milk. Mix well and let rest for 15 minutes. Stir with a fork to break up any lumps and let rest another 10 minutes. Mash banana and blend in agave and vanilla. Add banana mixture to the chia seed mixture and mix until well incorporated.

Place in refrigerator to set.

TO SERVE
Sprinkle with cinnamon.

Tip { Place all ingredients in a high-speed blender, adding meat from 1 Thai young coconut or ½ avocado, and blend. Add extra sweeter as desired.

Chocolate Caramel Bar—Four Layers

Bottom Chocolate Layer

You'll recognize this as the Simple Cacao Chocolate. Half of it will be used for the bottom layer of these bars, and half for the top. Will make approximately 2 cups.

1¾ cacao butter	¾ cup cacao powder
1 vanilla bean (do not use extract)	1 tablespoon agave
½ cup maple sugar powder or sucanat granules ground very fine in spice grinder	

Melt cacao butter in a double boiler.

Scrape seeds from vanilla bean and incorporate with the melting cacao butter.

In a large bowl, add cacao powder, melted cacao butter, salt, and powdered sweetener (do not add liquid sweetener or agave at this time).

Use a wire whisk and blend together until very smooth and all lumps are gone.

When smooth, taste for sweetness. Add agave or powdered sweetener to suit your taste; bitter chocolate or sweet, it's up to you.

Pour half the cacao mixture into an 8 × 8 square baking dish that has been lined with clear wrap, or use a square springform pan. Place in freezer. Set aside other half for the final step.

Second Layer

1 cup walnuts	7 medjool dates, soaked
⅛ cup dried coconut	1 teaspoon vanilla extract
2 tablespoons coconut oil, melted	¼ cup cacao nibs

Place nuts in food processor and pulse until nuts are small chunks. Add balance of ingredients and pulse-chop until crumbly and mixture stays together when pinched between your fingers. Remove chocolate bottom from freezer and spread second layer on top. Place back in freezer.

Third Layer

½ cup raw smooth peanut butter or almond butter	1 tablespoon maple syrup, or 1 tablespoon agave and ⅛ teaspoon maple extract combined
1 tablespoon coconut oil, melted	

Blend by hand; spread on top of second layer.

Fourth Layer

Use the second half of the chocolate recipe for this top layer If balance of chocolate has hardened, warm in a double boiler, stirring until smooth. If the chocolate is too thick, add a little more melted cacao butter and stir in. When the texture is right, pour on top of other layers and place back into the refrigerator to harden.

TO SERVE

Let sit out of the freezer for 10–15 minutes, and cut into squares with a very sharp knife. Store in refrigerator.

Do not use vanilla extract as it can make the cacao seize up and become stiff

Apple Pie

Very easy to make.

For the Crust

1½ cups macadamia nuts, soaked for 2 hours

1/½ cups walnuts or pecans, soaked for 2 hours

⅛ teaspoon Himalayan sea salt

Pulse in food processor until crumbled well. Do not overprocess, as the nuts will get too oily. Check as you pulse, scraping down sides. When mixture sticks together when pinched with your fingers, it's ready to put in your pie dish. Gently press in pie dish to form the crust.

For the Filling

- 4 cups dried apples, soaked in 2 cups apple juice to reconstitute
- 3 cups fresh apples, coarsely chopped and tossed with 1 tablespoon lemon juice
- 7 medjool dates, soaked until soft
- 2 oz. Irish moss gel, soaked overnight (see recipe on page 50)
- ½ teaspoon cinnamon
- ⅛ scant teaspoon nutmeg
- 1 tablespoon agave or maple syrup
- 1 teaspoon vanilla
- Pinch of Himalayan sea salt

You can make dried apples in your dehydrator or purchase organic naturally dried apples from the farmers' market, health food store, or online.

When apples are hydrated, strain juice to make Irish moss gel. Place chopped moss in blender with 1½ cups apple juice. Make more juice if necessary. Blend, adding water if needed to make a thick gel. Be sure the mixture is completely smooth and thick.

Place 3 cups chopped fresh apples, Irish moss gel, medjool dates, cinnamon, nutmeg, sweetener, vanilla, salt in a food processor and blend until smooth.

In food processor:

In a mixing bowl, combine apple mixture from food processor together with dried apples and blend with a spatula until well incorporated. Pour into piecrust.

For the Topping *(this makes the pie extra special)*

- 1 cup pecans, finely chopped
- 4 medjool dates, chopped fine
- ¼ teaspoon vanilla

Mix together to make a small chunky texture and crumble over top. Refrigerate pie to chill and set.

Baked Fruit

Use peach, apricot, nectarine, pear, or apple.

Cut fruit in half and remove the pit or seeds. Place fruit in a glass baking dish that will fit in your dehydrator. Sprinkle cinnamon and sweetener of choice, I like maple syrup or date syrup. Dehydrate for 3–4 hours until warm and slightly softened.

Serve with vanilla ice cream or eat warm for breakfast.

Three Pie Crusts

For one 8–9" pie or 4 tarts with removable bottoms. Crusts can be filled with fruits or puddings.

1. MACADAMIA NUTS

2-3 cups macadamia nuts, depending on size of pie dish or tart pans

⅛ teaspoon salt

Pulse nuts until broken down into small pieces. Do not overblend or they will get too oily. Pulse and check as you go along, scraping down sides until texture sticks together when pinched between your fingers. Pour into pie tart pans and lightly press in, bringing up the sides. It is ready to fill.

Choose fillings (see recipe on page 214).

2. CACAO CRUST

1½ cups walnuts

10-12 medjool dates

Dash of vanilla

1 tablespoon cacao powder

½ cup cacao nibs

1 tablespoon dried coconut flakes

Pinch of salt

Process all ingredients in food processor until it sticks together when pinched between your fingers. If it doesn't stick, add a teaspoon or two of water. Gently press into pie or tart pans. It is ready to fill.

Choose fillings (see recipe on page 214).

3. SIMPLE NUT CRUST

2 cups almonds, pecans, brazil, or walnuts

4-5 medjool dates

¼ cup coconut butter

Pinch of salt

Place nuts in a food processor and pulse-chop until small chunks form. Add dates one at a time through the feed tube while pulse-chopping. Add coconut butter, salt, and pulse-chop a few more times. If you can pinch the mixture between your fingers and it holds together, it is ready. If not, add another date or a tablespoon of water. Gently press into pie or tart pans.

Choose fillings (see recipe on page 214).

Fruit Pie Fillings

1½ cup lemon juice, Meyer lemons if possible

2 oz. Irish moss, made into a gel (see recipe on p. 50)

½ cup agave or sweetener of choice

1 tablespoon lecithin, ground in spice grinder

7 tablespoons coconut oil, melted in double boiler

2 baskets of berries or filling of choice, including raspberries, blueberries, peaches, strawberries, or kiwi

In food processor:

Place lemon juice, Irish moss gel, and sweetener, blending until smooth. Add lecithin and slowly pour melted coconut oil through feed tube while blending.

For large pie, incorporate ½ cup mashed berries with lemon, Irish moss mixture. If you are making 4 different tarts, mash 2 tablespoons each fruit and blend into ¼ of lemon, Irish moss mixture.

Fill tart pans with filling and top with whole fruits. Start by placing fruits in a full circle, starting from the outside rim and working around to the center, covering the complete top.

Chill to set in refrigerator.

Tip { Tarts can be cut into halves or quarters to serve.

Peach Cobbler

SERVES 8

Crust

3 cups macadamia nuts, soaked for 2 hours	⅛ teaspoon Himalayan sea salt

Pulse in food processor until it crumbles. Do not overprocess as the nuts will get oily. Check as you pulse, scraping down sides. Mixture is ready when it sticks together when pinched with your fingers. Gently press in pie dish to form the crust.

Filling

4 cups peaches, thinly sliced	1 oz. Irish moss, soaked overnight
5 medjool dates, soaked until soft	1 cup apple juice
1 tablespoon lemon juice	⅛ teaspoon cinnamon

Place sliced peaches in a bowl with 1 tablespoon lemon. Mix to incorporate and cover peaches.

Use juicer with blank blade to make date paste. Or blend in food processor with a drop or two of filtered water.

Chopped soaked Irish moss and place in blender. Add 1 cup apple juice and blend well, adding water if necessary to make a thick gel. Be sure the mixture is completely smooth.

Add 1 cup peaches, date paste, and Irish moss to your food processor. Pulse-chop until smooth.

Pour into bowl with remaining 3 cups of peaches and mix to incorporate ingredients.

Pour mixture into crust.

Topping

1 cup pecans	½ cups dates, soaked
1 tablespoon coconut butter, melted	Dash of vanilla

Place all ingredients in food processor and process until broken down and crumbly. Crumble over top of pie, sprinkle with cinnamon, and place in refrigerator to chill and set.

Tip { You can exchange peaches for apricots, mixed berries, or nectarines and choose any of the three crusts (see recipes on page 213).

Sweet Crepes

SWEET BANANA CREPE WRAP

Wraps can be filled with a variety of fruits and nut creams.

Meat from 7–8 Thai baby coconuts

1 banana, cut in half

½ cups cashews, soaked for 2 hours

2 oranges, juiced

2 dates, soaked and puréed

½ teaspoon vanilla extract or beans scraped from 1 vanilla bean

½ cup flaxseed, ground into a fine meal in spice or coffee grinder

½ water or more if needed

Blend all ingredients except flax meal and ½ orange juice in a high-speed blender, adding more juice as needed to make a smooth consistency. Add flax meal and more juice or water if needed. Blend until smooth and thick, but pourable. Taste and adjust for sweetness. Spread mixture on 2 nonstick dehydrator sheets an inch from the sides. Dehydrate for 4–5 hours at 110 degrees. Check to see if dry on top; if so, place a dehydrator mesh screen and tray on top of the crepes and flip over so the crepes are facedown on mesh tray. Remove original tray and peel off the nonstick sheet. Carefully help it along with a long knife to separate any sticky parts. Dehydrate another hour and cut each sheet into 4 parts. Dehydrate another hour until dry but pliable. Use immediately or store in a ziplock bag refrigerated for 3 days.

SWEET STRAWBERRY CREPE WRAP

Meat from 7–8 Thai baby coconuts

2 cups strawberries, washed and hulled

1 banana, cut in half

4 dates, soaked and puréed

½ teaspoon vanilla extract or beans scraped from 1 vanilla bean

¾ cup flaxseed, ground into a fine meal in spice or coffee grinder

Water

Blend all ingredients except flax meal and ½ orange juice in a high-speed blender, adding more juice as needed to make a smooth consistency. Add flax meal and more juice or water if needed. Blend until smooth and thick, but pourable. Taste and adjust for sweetness. Spread mixture on 2 nonstick dehydrator sheets an inch from the sides. Dehydrate for 4–5 hours at 110 degrees. Check to see if dry on top; if so, place a mesh dehydrator screen and tray on top of the crepes and flip over so the crepes are facedown on mesh tray. Remove original tray and peel off the nonstick sheet. Carefully help it along with a long knife to separate any sticky parts. Dehydrate another hour and cut each sheet into 4 parts. Dehydrate another hour until dry but pliable. Use immediately or store in a ziplock bag refrigerated for 3 days.

SWEET MANGO CREPE WRAP

Meat from 7–8 Thai baby coconuts	½ teaspoon vanilla extract or beans scraped from 1 vanilla bean
2 cups mango, chopped	
1 bananas, cut in half	¾ cup flaxseed, ground into a fine meal in spice or coffee grinder
4 dates, soaked and puréed	
	Water

Blend all ingredients except flax meal and ½ orange juice in a high-speed blender, adding more juice as needed to make a smooth consistency. Add flax meal and more juice or water if needed. Blend until smooth and thick, but pourable. Taste and adjust for sweetness. Spread mixture on 2 nonstick dehydrator sheets an inch from the sides. Dehydrate for 4–5 hours at 110 degrees. Check to see if dry on top; if so, place a dehydrator mesh screen and tray on top of the crepes and flip over so the crepes are facedown on mesh tray. Remove original tray and peel off the nonstick sheet. Carefully help it along with a long knife to separate any sticky parts. Dehydrate another hour and cut each sheet into 4 parts. Dehydrate another hour until dry but pliable. Use immediately or store in a ziplock bag refrigerated for 3 days.

Mike's Birthday BRAWnie

After a few tries at making a raw brownie to meet my boyfriend's standards, I finally arrived at a "thumbs-up." Served with vanilla ice cream, this is his special birthday cake. Although this brownie recipe has three parts, it is easy to make. The smells taunt you while the brownie is dehydrating.

Chocolate Mixture

1 cup almond milk (see recipe on p. 74)

½ cup cacao nibs

Handful of cashews, soaked 4 hours

Beans scraped from 1 vanilla pod, or 2 teaspoons
   vanilla extract

3 tablespoons agave or sweetener of choice

2–3 tablespoons filtered water

Blend until the nibs are broken up and the mixture is quite smooth. It should be a thick but pourable. Set aside.

Flour Mixture

15 medjool dates, soaked about 15 minutes until soft

4 tablespoon cacao powder

Pinch of Himalayan sea salt

4 cups walnut flour (This is made from soaking walnuts for 4 hours and dehydrating them overnight or until dry. Grind in a spice grinder or food processor to make into a flour consistency.)

2–3 tablespoons Irish moss gel or agar-agar (not raw)—I use Irish moss

¾ cup walnuts, coarsely chopped

Handful of raisins

Put dates in food processor and make into a smooth paste. Remove and place into a mixing bowl. To the bowl, add cacao powder, salt, Irish moss, 4 cups of walnut flour, chopped walnuts, and raisins. Mix well with a spatula or large spoon. Pour half of part 1 into the bowl and incorporate very well. Add balance a small amount at a time, incorporating until you reach dough consistency. It will look like standard brownie dough, which is creamy, dense, and spreadable. Taste for sweetness and add more if needed for your taste.

Divided mixture evenly onto 3 dehydrator screens into large squares about 1 inch thick. Wet a large flat knife with warm water to help smooth mixture flat.

Frosting

½ cup almond milk

¼ cup cacao nibs

2–3 tablespoons cacao powder

1 teaspoon vanilla extract

¼ cup agave or sweetener of choice

Pecan halves for topping

Blend almond milk, cacao nibs, cacao powder, vanilla, and sweetener until smooth. If thin, add a few cashews as a thickener and blend. If mixture is too thick, add more almond milk. Mixture should be on the thick side like a frosting. Taste for desired chocolate and sweetness and add more according to taste. Using a flat spatula, spread frosting on top of brownies, wetting spatula if needed. Press pecans on top of brownies and dehydrate at 115 for the first 2 hours, then turn down to 105 for another 6–8 hours or longer. Check with a toothpick to see if brownie is the texture you like. Brownies will have a slight crust on the outside and a softer center. Texture is personal preference.

Tip { You can stack two or three squares to make a cake and put filling of fruit in between each layer, or cut into small squares.

Blackberry Cheesecake with Maple Cream Topping

For the Crust

2 cups of pecans

5 tablespoons cacao nibs

3 tablespoons cacao powder

Pinch of salt

Dash of vanilla

5 medjool dates, pitted

Put all ingredients in food processor except dates. Pulse until chopped. Add dates one at a time through the feed tube and pulse until incorporated, leaving bit of a chunk. Pinch a piece between your fingers; if it sticks together, it is finished.

Press the crust into a springform pan (or pie plate lined with clear wrap), bringing up the sides about ½ to 1 inch. Place several whole blackberries spaced around the sides about 2–3 inches apart. Set aside. Blackberries make it pretty design on the outside when the rim is removed from the springform pan.

For the Blackberry Syrup and decoration

3 cups blackberries plus one cup, reserved for decoration

Blend blackberries in blender. Add a little sweetener to taste. Strain mixture through strainer to separate the blackberry seeds. You might have to stir the mixture to move the seeds aside and help the liquid to pass through the strainer. Pour in a container and set aside.

For the Cheesecake Filling

3 cups soaked cashews

2 cups almond milk

Juice from ½ lemon

⅓ cup agave or sweetener of choice

Pinch of salt

Dash of vanilla

1 cup plus 2 tablespoons coconut oil

¼ cup sunflower lecithin or Irish moss gel

Blend the cashews, almond milk, lemon, sweetener, vanilla, and salt in blender. While blender is running, slowly add the melted coconut oil, and, if you are using it, the lecithin.

Remove ⅓ of the mixture to a container and stir in 1 tablespoon of maple extract or maple syrup. Taste for sweetness and set aside. If preferred, use maple extract mixed with agave instead of maple syrup. This is your maple cream topping.

Add blackberry syrup to the balance of the mixture still in blender. Blend and taste for sweetness.

Pour ½ the mixture into the crust, drizzle maple syrup over the top and tap the mold to settle the filling. Add balance of the blackberry mixture and tap again. Place in the freezer for 15–20 minutes.

Remove from freezer and top with the maple cream topping.

Place cheesecake back in freezer for 4-5 hours.

TO SERVE

Take cheesecake from the freezer 10–15 minutes before serving and remove the springform pan.

Drizzle maple syrup on top and spread across the whole top with a spatula or flat knife. This helps to hold the berries in place. Place halved pecans around the outside circumference. Decorate with whole blackberries placed around in a circle to cover top. I like to serve when center is slightly frozen.

TO SERVE

Drizzle maple syrup and blackberry sauce around the plate of individual serving.

Resources

ENVIRONMENTAL GROUPS, ENLIGHTENING BOOKS, RAW FOOD MAGAZINES, INFORMATIVE FILMS, AND RAW FOOD RESTAURANTS

Eating raw food changes your life in other ways besides feeling physical fit, energetic, and happy. Many of my raw food friends reveal they became more aware of where their food came from. They started thinking about who planted the seeds and who nurtured its growth and who picked the fruit when it was ready for market.

As I drive by farms in northern California and see hundreds of farmworkers bending over in the fields, sun beating down on their heads, I appreciate and respect what it takes to grow food and bring it to our table. When I visit organic farms around the country and see the care taken to grow vegetables without chemicals or pesticides, I know what a giant step these farmers are taking to bring us the best-tasting chemical-free food possible. They have my complete admiration and respect.

Many of my friends, including myself, have vegetable gardens and enjoy the most tasty and beautiful-looking vegetables all year round by freezing the bounty when necessary for winter months. It's wonderful news to learn more families are tending home or community gardens than in past years.

When we start to eat for health, we gain increased consciousness of our ecosystem. We become aware of chemicals and pesticides used in growing food, cleaning supplies, and beauty products. We begin to realize we have the power to make a difference in the products we buy and whom we buy them from.

Being a raw foodist is similar to becoming vegetarian decades ago. Not many knew what it was or the reason for being a vegetarian. Vegetarianism has grown over the years. Most everyone is conscious of vegetarian food into today's society. In India, an estimated 40% of the population are vegetarians.

I believe eating raw food will become very popular in years to come. It will be commonplace to find raw food restaurants and raw food choices on menus and in markets. There already are some fantastic raw food restaurants and I've eaten at many of them, including Pure Food and Wine, New York; Quintessence, New York; Café Gratitude, San Francisco, California; Cru, Los Angeles, California; Karyn's Raw, Chicago, Illinois; Planet Raw, Santa Monica, California; Au Lac, Fountain Valley, California; 118 Degrees, Costa Mesa, California; Euphoria Loves Rawvolution, Santa Monica, California; The Greenery, Encinitas, California; Sun Power Natural Café, Studio City, California; LifeFood Organics, Hollywood, California; 105Degrees, Oklahoma City; Java Green, Washington, DC, and KindKream, a vegan, raw, organic desert shop in Studio City, California

Raw magazines I recommend; *Purely Delicious* and *Get Fresh*. Be sure to Google a couple of my raw food heroes; Phillip McCluskey and Angela Stokes. I think you will be impressed by their accomplishments eating a raw food diet.

Consciousness about our environment is another added bonus when eating raw foods. It makes sense as environmental issues are tied closely to the foods we eat and the water we drink. I was honored to be invited to board the Riverkeeper boat on a recent tour of the Hudson River in upstate New York. The Riverkeeper is a non profit organization whose mission is to protect the ecological integrity of the Hudson River and its tributaries, and to safeguard the drinking water supply of 9 million New Yorkers. They cruise up and down the river daily looking for polluters and they are working to close down the looming Indian Point Nuclear Power Plant in favor of cleaner, safer energy.

In the '80s, I was involved with the Environmental Media Association (EMA) whose mission is to mobilize the entrainment industry in a global effort to educate people about environmental issues and inspire them into action.

Important environmental non profit groups include World Wildlife Fund, Greenpeace International, National Geographic Society, Friends of the Earth, National Wildlife Federation, Ecology Fund.com, National Audubon Society, and TreePeople. Films including *The 11th Hour* and *Who Killed the Electric Car* might be of interest to you. You also might want to check out:

http://www.gliving.com–For all news green

http://livingwithed.net/–Green home television show

http://www.peta.org/–Learn more about animal protection

Books I recommend: *Eat To Live* by Dr. Joel Fuhrman, *The China Study* by Dr. T. Colin Campbell, *The World Peace Diet* by Will Tuttle, *Omnivore's Dilemma* by Michael Pollan, and *Eating Animals* by Jonathan Safran Foer.

A few films to educate yourself regarding animals and the food we eat include *Earthlings*, *Food Inc.*, *The Cove*, *FoodMatters*, and *Fresh*.

Acknowledgments and Thanks

Writing a book cannot be done alone. I've had so much support and love along the way. No words can truly express how I feel about my boyfriend of eight years, Michael Mendell, who always gives me his constant support. Whether I called on him to take photos of food I styled at midnight or six o'clock in the morning, he was there by my side. When I asked him to taste endless desserts, he obliged. He read my manuscript, made suggestions, and helped me with my grammar. He looked after me at every step of the way. He made sure I got up from my desk chair to stretch or take a break to sit in the sun. He made sure that I had the proper light to work with, and he chauffeured me to farmers' markets and health food stores all over the city. His calmness kept me balanced through long periods of writing. His photos grace the pages of this book, and I've been graced by his kindness and love.

My family makes me feel special by always supporting my many transformations. Their encouragement is endless and their love enduring. Thank you to my children, Lisa, Jonas, Mia, and Dan; my inspiring grandchildren, Mackenzie, Hannah, Luke, Audrey, Karly, Rocco, and Gunner; and to my daughter-in-laws, Toni and Gigi. You all know how much you mean to me, and how much I love you. I appreciate all your help and patience while I wrote this book.

Thanks to Sarma Meingaillis for all her support, encouragement, and for sharing her connections. Thanks to my friends Susan Santilena, Lori Clayton-Temple, and Mary French for helping me test recipes in my tiny kitchen. Thanks to Kari Stuart, my agent, for looking out for me every step of the way, and to Ann Treisman, my editor, for all her work in making sure everything came together beautifully and timely. And thanks to Skyhorse Publishing for accepting my manuscript and to everyone there who worked on this project.

Big hugs and thanks to my wonderful talented friend Michael Keller, who took the professional photos of me in his kitchen, and who kept Mike and I entertained and fed from his amazing garden while doing the shoot. Thanks to Barbara Fletcher, Wendy Burt-Thomas, and Robin Strober for helping to look over my scribbling. And hugs to Barry Blau for his keen eye. Much gratitude goes to my longtime best friend, Julie Kavner, for always believing in me and cheering me on in all my endeavors for so many years.

People for the Ethical Treatment of Animals (PETA) deserve big thanks for all the work they do. I owe them thanks or putting me in the spotlight, which inspired me to write this book. And last but not least, my growing list of Facebook friends who encouraged me to write this book. From different parts of the world, in many languages, I've been supported and blessed with caring friends. The kindest words and well wishes have come from people I've never met in person. I've been told I've changed their lives, but in fact, my Facebook friends have changed mine.

Index

Skyhorse Publishing books may be purchased in bulk at special discounts for sales promotion, corporate gifts, fund-raising, or educational purposes. Special editions can also be created to specifications. For details, contact the Special Sales Department, Skyhorse Publishing, 307 West 36th Street, 11th Floor, New York, NY 10018 or info@skyhorsepublishing.com.

Skyhorse® and Skyhorse Publishing® are registered trademarks of Skyhorse Publishing, Inc.®, a Delaware corporation.

www.skyhorsepublishing.com

10 9 8 7 6 5 4 3 2

Library of Congress Cataloging-in-Publication Data is available on file.

ISBN: 978-1-61608-274-1

Printed in China